WITHDRAWN

DATE DUE

OCT 1 5 2007
AUG 1 2 2010
SEP 1 2 2011
JUL 2 8 2015
JUL 2 9 2015
AUG 1 8 2015

BRODART, CO.   Cat. No. 23-221-003

D1318935

Launch Your Career in College

Launch Your Career in College

Strategies for Students, Educators, and Parents

Adele M. Scheele

Foreword by Alexander W. Astin

Westport, Connecticut
London

Library of Congress Cataloging-in-Publication Data

Scheele, Adele M.
  Launch your career in college : strategies for students, educators, and
parents / Adele M. Scheele ; foreword by Alexander W. Astin.
      p. cm.
  Includes bibliographical references and index.
  ISBN 0-275-98512-1 (alk. paper)
  1. College student orientation. 2. College students—Vocational
guidance. 3. College students—Employment. 4. Career development.
5. Business networks. 6. School-to-work transition. I. Title.
  LB2343.3.S32 2005
  378.1'98—dc22   2005018684

British Library Cataloguing in Publication Data is available.

Library of Congress Catalog Card Number: 2005018684
ISBN: 0-275-98512-1

First published in 2005

Praeger Publishers, 88 Post Road West, Westport, CT 06881
An imprint of Greenwood Publishing Group, Inc.
www.praeger.com

Printed in the United States of America

The paper used in this book complies with the
Permanent Paper Standard issued by the National
Information Standards Organization (Z39.48-1984)

10 9 8 7 6 5 4 3 2 1

To my husband, Mercer David Distler

Contents

Chapter 8: Finding Your First Job 125

Chapter 9: Success Plan for Your College Years 159

Chapter 10: Making the Transition 171

Recommended Reading 185

Index 187

Foreword

One of the common mistakes that prospective college students make is to assume a passive stance toward their college experience: "What can this college do for me?" Adele Scheele's basic message in this lively and informative book is a very different and empowering one: "What can I do that will enrich my college experience and enhance my career development?"

Taking a proactive stance toward one's higher education experience not only opens doors and widens one's range of options; it also changes the individual by developing new knowledge, new skills, and new perspectives. Scheele thus likens the college and graduate school experience to a kind of laboratory, where the student uses all of the available resources—people, programs, and facilities—as tools for learning and creating opportunities.

In putting forward her many creative suggestions for how to take charge of your own higher education experience, Scheele makes an important point that most students are probably only vaguely aware of: our educational system tends to encourage student passivity and conformity through its regimented system of uniform curricular requirements, course assignments, testing, and grading. Classroom teachers are well aware of this problem, whereby many students seem content merely to comply with whatever it is that they think their instructor expects—no more, no less.

Scheele's basic point is that this kind of passivity and compliance on the part of the student represents a wasted opportunity to learn, develop, and prepare for the future beyond college.

Scheele's many specific suggestions can be especially valuable for commuter students and for that substantial majority of college students who attend large public institutions. Thus, while passive or reticent students who attend small private residential colleges may be "noticed" by fellow students or by faculty or staff, who might subsequently encourage them to become more engaged, such students can spend four or five years attending a large public institution, not have any significant interaction either with student peers or with institutional personnel, and not be noticed by anyone.

If there is a single, fundamental principle that informs Scheele's wide-ranging advice, it would be to cultivate relationships, not just with fellow students, but also with professors, advisors, administrators, recruiters, and professionals in the field. The opportunities for initiating and nurturing such relationships are everywhere: the classroom, the private office, meetings, workshops, job interviews, social and cultural events, volunteer work, and the many dozens of student organizations that one finds on the typical campus.

While most of the book is devoted to showing students how to get the most out of the college experience, Chapter 8 nicely complements the other chapters by providing extremely useful information concerning how to go about finding a job. Among the many critical topics covered are résumés, application letters, references, and that most critical of all events—the job interview. Even people who are decades beyond their college years could benefit from reading this chapter.

While Scheele has wisely made this book readily accessible to the reader by avoiding the use of distracting footnotes and references, much of what she is recommending has, in fact, been supported by systematic research on college students. Thus, when she speaks of the benefits to be derived from such diverse experiences as membership in student organizations, volunteer service, and internships and when she advises the student to forge close connections with other students and with professors, there is a considerable body of empirical research evidence to back her up. Indeed, perhaps the most important practical generalization to be derived from the many hundreds of studies that have been done on college students is right at the heart of Scheele's wise counsel: if you want to get the most of our your college experience, get involved.

Alexander W. Astin, PhD
Allan M. Cartter Professor Emeritus
of Higher Education
Founding Director,
Higher Education Research Institute
University of California, Los Angeles

Preface

This book is a guide to finding yourself in college by being active and not just letting things happen. I have included inspiring stories of highly successful people whose college lives, by their own admission, were not so clearly defined at the beginning. Yet, they made their way through the sometimes unplanned or chaotic process to find intellectual challenges, connections, and opportunities that led them to realize their passionate pursuits, their callings. You, too, can learn college success skills that will allow you to learn how to identify your talents and passions and find direction from mentors, assignments, and projects. You can make college even more significant than you ever dared to dream.

I understand college from every side now. I learned each time I enrolled as a student—earning a BS, an MA, and then a PhD. I learned from teaching in high school and college and from conducting corporate training programs. I learned from interviewing achievers about their college and professional experiences and from my career-coaching clients, who shared their achievements and frustrations. For years I have been regularly giving presentations to business organizations, encouraging their members to live more productively and purposefully, and to college classes, teaching students to think about how to "use" college in the largest sense possible.

My intention is so much greater than simply helping you pass your courses, get good grades, or just do adequate work. I hope that you will learn to develop the life skills that will enable you, too, to work and live more meaningfully. After all, it is the reason you are coming to college and investing your time, money, and hope.

College sounds so simple: apply, get accepted, and fulfill your requirements. However, that is less than half the story of the glory that you can find in college—if you are willing. Too often, students miss out. Even smart students misuse their college years. Let me show you the profound difference between being just a good student and being an adventurous, proactive student. By choosing proactivity, you open yourself to the transforming power of college and graduate school. Higher education offers you the chance to have quality time with professors—great thinkers whose brilliance can direct or redirect your lives. College is a time to forge such relationships. It is a time to experiment with ideas and leadership in clubs, activities, and new programs. It is the truest training ground. College can be a catalyst for your life, if you pursue it that way, and if you are willing to be active and give up a more passive role of just following instructions.

I hope you are listening. I hope you will think about the ideas in this book and try them. If you do, you are bound to change your life for the good, even for the great! Because I have made finding your calling my own passionate calling, think of me as your coach, and allow each chapter to act as a session. I welcome your experiences.

Acknowledgments

I am lucky to have Susan Slesinger, Praeger Publishers' Editor, as a true friend. She is not only a brilliant editor, but she is also encouraging and empathetic, a rare combination. And she shares my profound belief that the ideas in this book deserve to live.

I also have had the good fortune to have Ann Morey, my genius successor as director of Cal State Northridge's career center, at my side for nine years. She has enthusiastically joined me in extending the notion that a student can transform a meager life of waiting in line for life to happen into the adventure of an explorer of all that college can offer. Victor Diamante has been my computer savior, guru, and formatter; I hired him as a part-time tech assistant when he was a freshman, and now he works full-time in a larger department. Technologically intuitive, he has never, ever let me down. Thanks, too, to Nancy Worsham, who gathered student FAQs and helped put ideas in order.

I am indebted to great friends whose support has meant so much. Millie Loeb has always been a source of strength and ready repartee on the promise of books, college, politics, and work. Nancy Hathaway, a writer herself, read my manuscript at the eleventh hour and buoyed me up with her enthusiasm for these ideas, which do not usually appear in college books. Janet Albaugh, with her succinct and precise knowledge and style, turned endless lists into paragraphs and helped reorganize ideas.

In my own college experience, enrolling in three academic programs, each seven years apart, I sought out the best professors I could find. I was rewarded every time. In ways they will never know, each of them inspired me and helped shape my life. Here are just some of their names to share with you: at the University of Pennsylvania's undergraduate program, Woody Woodhouse, Moshe Greenberg, and Morse Peckam; at Cal State Northridge's Graduate English Fellowship, Harry Stone and Ann Stanford; and at UCLA in the Change Management Doctoral Fellowship, Helen S. Astin, a courageous and inspiring mentor, who chaired my dissertation committee and became a lifelong friend.

Finally, here's to students everywhere, who might turn college into a catalyst and make it their own personal laboratory to discover the ways that brilliant professors, exciting programs, and chance events can transform their future by opening and expanding new vistas, opportunities, and dreams.

Chapter 1
Transforming the
College Experience

Education is not filling a bucket but lighting a fire.
—William Butler Yeats

College is an experiment in hope. It is also a risky investment of thousands of dollars and many years of study. Whether it is a matter of graduate or undergraduate school, a 2-year or an 8-year program—the 2000 Current Population Survey found that fifteen million people dedicate part of their lives to attending college. For the time and money spent, students rightly expect a great return in the form of a professional career. Having a college degree makes students nearly 40% more likely to gain access to jobs of importance and allows for quick career advancement beyond the entry level. Still, we expect even more: a ticket to the outside world and an enhanced identity.

MAKING THE MOST OF YOUR GREAT EXPECTATIONS

Here's an example of someone who was a good student and did everything she thought was right. But she couldn't find a job after she graduated and thought she had wasted her college experience. This, like all the stories included in this book, is a true story.

Suzie's Story: Voulez-Vouz Fries with That?

Suzie was used to getting As. She graduated at the top of her small liberal arts college class with a BA in French—went to class and studied by day, and waited tables at a local coffee shop at night. Suzie hoped that a job in Paris, the city of her dreams, would be hers after graduation. Near the end of her last semester, Suzie mailed out dozens of letters requesting job information, but she didn't get a single response. To her disappointment, Suzie discovered that getting employment overseas with an American company was a plum assignment given as a reward to those who were already working in that company. There were two other alternatives open to her—teaching or applying to graduate school—but she didn't want to do either. Depressed, Suzie felt that college had been a complete failure, a waste of her time and money.

But it didn't have to be like that at all. Suzie's major was definitely not wasted: studying another language and culture is, in itself, profoundly valuable. It's just not enough. By not *using* college in an active, engaging way, Suzie failed to uncover and create valuable opportunities. While she was not totally passive, she was *unimaginative*. Just think of what she could have done while she was in college to chart her path to Paris if she had thought of the following opportunities.

1.   She could have gotten to know her French professors by talking to them during office hours and/or by working for them. They might, in turn, find interesting projects for her and connect her to potential employers.

2.   She could have chosen a French import business as a project and/or written a paper about it, interviewing some key people who might have led her to an exciting career.

3.   She could have volunteered at the French consulate, making contacts for future friendships or networking.

4.   She could have worked as a translator at the mayor's office in her college town and may have found a variety of prospects.

5.   She could have worked part time at a bank based in France, getting exposure to people doing business there.

6.   She could have waited tables at a French restaurant rather than a coffee shop, connecting herself to a French chef or owner and even French customers or suppliers.

7.   She could have developed her leadership skills by joining the French club and becoming an officer and inviting French artists, politicians, and business people to campus. Great leads might have come through these contacts.

8.   She could have spent her junior year in France, working or volunteering part time for an American company with offices in Paris. This might have led to a job offer after graduation.

Pursuing these projects and cocurricular activities would have taken time, courage, research, and energy. But any one of them would have paid off for Suzie with more than just the job she was looking for. These explorations would have developed her sense of courage and maybe even ignited some passion for a way to use her talents. It certainly would have been a lot more fun. These opportunities could have been building blocks to construct her future—and perhaps a passport to Paris, as well as into her heart. How might this kind of thinking work for you in your major? What could you do now?

You can apply these imaginative activities to enhance what you are required to do and the major you have chosen. This book is about your taking action in college where you thought you should be passive. But there is every chance for you to be proactive. For example, use test-taking or paper-writing as ways to learn about successful people, great companies, professional fields, or challenging ideas. You can stimulate and discover your own interests so that your dreams have a chance of being fulfilled. Combining your curriculum with your life is a great way to create a set of goals that lead to self-discovery.

Dare to experience college as your own *laboratory*, not as an isolated ivory tower. In order to do that, you have to view college as a source of people, contacts, ideas, power, creativity, and opportunity. If you do, you'll find that the real possibilities of college can be as open-ended as you are open-minded and willing to take risks. It requires exploration of what is yet unknown to you but is beckoning. Change is scary; be brave.

When it comes down to it, you are the one who figures out how to "use" college. It can be either a continuation of merely fulfilling other people's assignments, a time-out from the real world, or it can be a head start into the real world as you create it and contribute to it. It is what you make it. And through your college experience, you shape your future self.

We usually assume that we just have to register for classes, show up regularly, do our assignments, and then the rewards will all come—we will begin a rewarding life. We expect to be made acceptable, valuable, knowledgeable, and finally prepared for graduate school or immediate professional employment. We also assume that by graduation, everything will suddenly become clear: we will find our callings automatically and then have a guarantee for a successful career. This expectation, seldom conscious, lies deep in our hearts. We expect the promise will be fulfilled, but we don't know how.

> *Nothing will work*
> *unless you do.*
> *—Maya Angelou*

Using College as Your Laboratory for Self-Discovery

I have counseled thousands of people who once had faith in this magic. All of them had wanted something to happen to them after they had enrolled in college or signed up for a course; all of them had been keenly disappointed when the expected alchemy didn't take place. It took them years to discover that, when all you do is show up, such a transformation doesn't *just happen*. You have to *actively make it happen*. You went crazy trying to get accepted into college—now you need to make college yield an intellectual, social, and vocational life.

If you believe in magic, then you must learn to become the magician. You are the only one who can turn yourself into what you want to be—even if, at the beginning, you don't know what that is. If you are really smart, you will want a lot more for yourself than merely making the grade, getting a degree, and finding a job. Don't be satisfied with just going to college and getting several years older, unless you are content to sleepwalk through life. Learn to recognize your *passivity*—whether it's a little or a lot—and *avoid it*. Instead, use the time for all it's worth. You're paying for it—make it pay off. College is the ideal time to explore opportunities for the future.

You explore life by participating in it and by making it as intellectual, creative, and fulfilling as you can through a process of change, experimentation, belonging, and contributing. The journey will be both painful and joyous.

Unlearning Dependency on the System

Why is life so hard? The odd thing is that we haven't been taught how to live life, only to follow the plan. We are full of many "lifeless" lessons. We have all been conditioned—brainwashed, really—to wait passively for things to happen to us *instead of making things happen*. If you think you have escaped this conditioning, think again. Most of us learned as early as seventh grade that we would pass, and even excel, if we just did the work assigned to us by our teachers. Here is how we learned that. Remember asking whether the test covered all of chapter five or only a part of it? Whether the assigned paper should be ten pages long or thirty? Whether you'd get extra credit for two book reports on two books by the same author or two books written in the same period? But what were you really learning? You were learning the *formula*:

- Find out what's expected.
- Do it as well as you can.
- Wait for the grade.

And the formula always worked. You got good grades. But take a second look to understand what that process actually means. Yes, you took tests, wrote papers, got passing grades, and then were automatically promoted from one year to the next in elementary, junior, and senior high school. If you do what is asked, you are taken care of. You never have to compete for promotions. You never have to rehearse yourself or even persuade anyone to move you forward. It happens *automatically*. You never learn to *stretch*. We get used to *system dependency!* What does it cost? If doing what's expected is all you do, the cost is that you learn only to fill orders. Change that now. The same thing can happen in college and even in graduate or professional school unless you expand your expectations. Only in this way will you come alive. Discard the formula.

College: More Than You Expected (If You're Not Passive!)

Once learned, system dependency lies deep within us, unconscious, behind our eyelids, muzzling our brain. It doesn't change when we graduate, but lurks inside and rules our life, keeping us back from being our best selves. Rather than learning the subject *in our heart*, we've learned it *by heart*. And that makes all the difference between feeling fraudulent and feeling alive.

You can change everything if your attitude is to *expect more*. Once you find that studying history or art or anthropology can be much more than just obediently following orders, your academic pursuits can lead you to new worlds of experiences, courses, contacts, and later, *careers*.

If you could describe your own expectations of college before you set foot on campus and compare that to what you actually experience, you might be as surprised as the many students who responded to an online survey. In that survey, as many students were disappointed that college was less intellectually challenging than they had expected as those students who found it to be more challenging than they had expected. More than half of those responding expected that college would be a difficult place to make friends.

Disappointment in college comes from misusing college, by treating it as *school* instead of *life*. To reframe your attitude, train yourself to approach college in the same positive, productive, active way that most successful people approach their careers, and in the very same way they approached college. Success is a result of taking charge of your life, including college, far beyond *just passively accepting* what is put before you.

BECOMING AN ADULT:
TRANSITIONING FROM HIGH SCHOOL TO COLLEGE

You may feel overwhelmed by the new freedom that college offers. It will even be frighteningly chaotic. No wonder! Your life in high school was completely regimented by the teachers who gave daily assignments and expected you to accommodate. College will seem the polar opposite, because it gives you a very wide choice of how much to comply. Although you might have only two exams for a course, or one paper, don't be fooled into thinking that's all there is to it. You will be expected to do much more: actively participate in class discussions, read the required assignments, review lectures, and go over lab results. Such expectations will usually be stated only once, if at all. You may find that, for the first time, your educational environment is treating you like an *adult* and assuming that you will take complete responsibility for your part. Once you realize that, you can grow into it.

Being suddenly on your own will require your sense of discipline to emerge so that you can manage study time, time with friends, and even work time. For many students, this in itself requires a steep learning curve. It is like being thrown into the deep end of the pool. Too many temptations arise—from overdoing parties and drugs to goofing off or hiding out. But unlike swimming, surviving and thriving in the college environment consists largely of adopting a purposive attitude rather than only learning a specific skill.

SKILLS, GOALS, LOVE (!), AND THIS BOOK

The main purpose of this book is to help you acquire a positive, *nonpassive* attitude. I recommend highlighting passages that seem particularly useful and writing all over the margins. This will make the book intimately *yours* as well as help you absorb and remember it. If you do it right, you will begin the practice of being proactive in every course and in every aspect of your college life.

College is your time for learning skills that you will use for the rest of your life, skills that will serve you far beyond your major or your degree, skills that will make you successful. It can yield so much more than you imagine. It will be a time for exploring new subjects, discovering who you are, finding your strengths, igniting your interests, and developing skills. College is the time for accomplishing goals. It's a time to fall in love with ideas and people; many will stay with you throughout your entire life. Expect miracles when you practice these skills.

I try to act as if I make a difference.
—William James

CAN GETTING A'S BE BAD FOR YOU?

I have discovered a clear pattern of success through my work as a career strategist. I have both coached a great variety of people: teachers, bankers, artists, entrepreneurs, executives, scientists, professors, lawyers, and other professionals who wanted to be, or who already were, successful at what they do. I have mapped their lives, connected the dots of their innate or discovered passions, found how they decided on majors, how they used college, and how they forged impressive careers. Over and over again, I found that people who became successful in their careers learned these skills for success by practicing them when they were active in college. Here's what I found.

Active means more than only busy and engaged—active means *not passive*. Successful people found clues to their own interests by paying attention to what courses interested them and following up on that material. They all found professors who would become critical mentors to them during and after college. Their mentors pointed out careers and opportunities that they might not have thought of and connected them to researchers and prospective employers in graduate school or directly in a career. They also joined clubs and activities that appealed to them (sometimes even on a whim) and did what really interested them. They used their talents effectively. They made their studies and their activities comprise their identity, far more than an average college student would.

I know. I found that those who became stuck or frustrated in their careers were those who had a negative mindset in college. It was as if they were holding themselves back, feeling as if they were not worthy, somehow afraid to become involved in their subjects or with their professors. Not only were they unaware that *they* were sabotaging *themselves*, they thought quite the opposite—that they were in fact being "fair" by not selling out, being too pushy, or sucking up. They simply were waiting to be recognized for their smartness and then directed on to a certain path.

They were in a self-imposed holding pattern. They were living out a false idea of being "good."

Avoiding the "Good Student" Trap

I call this mindset the *"Good Student" Trap*. Here "good" means obedient, rather than the opposite of bad. In this context, "good" means just waiting passively for good grades and nothing much else. We are taught to do only what is expected of us, racking up our accomplishments from the list of others' expectations—not our own. And then, even if we do an exceptional job of fulfilling those expectations, we are conditioned to wait and wait and wait—first for our schoolteachers, then for our professors, and later for our bosses to grade, direct, and praise our work, and then promote us automatically to the next level. When did getting something *automatically* improve your self-respect?

Being Recognized (or Not!) and Your Development

From my clients' lives, I learned something quite unexpected. School implicitly follows a particular power structure: one professor leads a class of students, all equally unempowered. The one ultimate authority dispenses instruction and assignments to them. How, then, do students go about getting attention, direction, and recognition when they are in this serf-like position? The answer determines which students will succeed.

First of all, achievers learn to get attention by doing good work, but they don't stop there. They also learn to build relationships and build on their interests. Achievers love what they do and do it well. In college, they learned to take themselves seriously. They never gave up having fun, but they started in college to learn what motivated and excited them. They became apprentices to people who, in turn, became their mentors. And then they grew into masters of their craft. These same ways are the ways you can begin the process of forging your identity and finding your purpose in college. This process turns black and white life into vivid Technicolor. Yes, it takes the extra effort of figuring out how to really fly by escaping your own preconceptions, but it's worth it.

Seventh Grade, Part Deux?

System dependency is not the only damaging concept you learned in school. You also learned your *place*—unnatural groups of a single age behaving obediently. Think back to the life-shaping lessons you learned from your middle school or junior high cafeteria. As seventh graders, you couldn't eat with eighth graders; they wouldn't let you. You'd be labeled brain-damaged if you invited your teacher to sit with you. But you probably didn't sit with just any seventh graders either; you preferred those who looked like you, acted like you, and came from families like yours. You blocked out everyone who was different, and you were locked out in turn. You learned to think that this was how life was. What a mistaken idea!

You wouldn't be caught dead going after the attention of your teachers. You'd be labeled an apple-polisher or worse, so you didn't do it. Instead, you cut yourself off from opportunity by holding back from volunteering, starting a new activity, or following up on some idea that interested you. It would have been great if you had a mentor, someone to inspire you—but by not talking to your teachers, you did not give yourself the chance.

What you couldn't know was that students who would become successful in their careers were students who were recognized, rewarded, mentored, and given valuable support and opportunities to explore. It may have seemed like luck was favoring those students, but I found that they were active in their classes, clubs, and activities. Whether purposefully or not, they created a learning environment that also included building relationships that regular students didn't even know existed. Most of these successful students learned many different things that would keep them in good stead all their lives—from gaining the intellectual content of the courses, to being the one referred on to more challenging projects, to understanding how to connect to professors, sponsors, coaches, and even friends. But far too many students were lulled into a false sense of self-labeled "good" because they merely fulfilled the expected curriculum. The alternative, they thought, was being "bad"—feeling alienated and losing interest or dropping out. There is so much more to learn by rethinking what you are doing so that your actions work for you. You need to take control of what you are doing. You have to start now.

Why settle for college becoming a sequel to high school, just with older students and tougher assignments? Instead, reframe it in your mind so that it resembles a place where you can be so much more alive in a complex, responsive world that invites your contribution. Ironically, the longer you passively wait for life to favor you, the more you will become invisible. Your self-esteem will suffer. Your imagination will not develop.

Sadly, the "good student" attitude can actually block you from becoming motivated and connected to new ideas and networks of people. Doing only what is asked of you, even though you may do it perfectly, is a gross misunderstanding of what college is all about! You only get several years older and deeper in debt.

Fear of Failing and How It Can Wreck You

Yes, you certainly do have to get good grades on tests. Colleges demand more than a decent GPA from high school as proof that you can and will perform. In this same way, high academic standing in college becomes a prime indicator to potential employers of your ability to perform on the job. So it makes sense that tests remain the standard for measuring performance in college. Yet, who likes taking exams? They always create anxiety. They are not always fair. They don't always seem to measure accurately what you know about your subject. And you don't often learn or remember anything after the memorization process. But you still have to live with them—a lot of them.

One big problem is fear. *Fear of failing.* Fear of not being as smart as you're supposed to be. You start thinking about life as a test, judged and branded by an Authority, that you will either pass or fail. You may start feeling afraid that you will fail even before you do, if you do. In fact, most of the time you don't fail; you're just mortally afraid that you're going to. Unfortunately, if you don't do as well as you wish, you usually don't get a second chance to prove yourself or raise your grade. If you do perform well, you may think that you somehow got away with something this time, but you may worry that next time they will discover that you are a fraud. Gradually, just the fear of being found out can ruin your life, because when you are afraid, you lose your curiosity and originality, your talent and your spirit—your life spirit. But there are strategies to cut short fear, reclaim yourself, and at the same time, boost your self-esteem and courage.

PRACTICE EXPERIMENTING: EXERCISE YOUR IMAGINATION

Consider the creative process of a scientific experiment. First, you develop your hypothesis. Then, you test it. If it works, you feel great because you were right all along and proved your theory. But you haven't actually learned much because you already suspected it.

Suppose, however, that you don't prove what you set out to do. At first, you would be disappointed. You were wrong, but have you *failed?* Only if you think the experiment is *a test.* If you think that, then getting an unexpected answer is a failure. Many people decide to quit then and there, whether it's a chemistry project or an archeological dig. What scientists learn is to try another approach, and that is what we all should do. Follow their example. Go on, in genuine experimental fashion; restructure your hypothesis, reexamine your variables, try another approach, and apply your own educated hunches. Only by actively exerting yourself do you discover things you didn't know before. Science, like most other worthwhile activities, is rarely pursued without imagination.

What exactly is imagination? Imagination is finding our own response to an idea or following some innate reason or flash of insight. Following our true "North Star" may guide each of us to develop a direction of interests into a passionate pursuit. How do you begin? Just sign up to do something you might want to do—writing poetry or composing songs or playing soccer or meeting inventors. Use your imagination when you read the campus newspaper and bulletin boards for lists of activities and opportunities, and hope for a green light to go on inside you. Don't discount anything by thinking "Why should I get involved in that? It's not one of my interests." Instead, consider "Why shouldn't I look into that? It might lead to something new, even if just more contacts." Imagination leads to opportunities.

Too many of us let limited self-esteem get in our way. Instead of feeling that "They won't be interested in me," try to think, "I have as much to offer as most others." With such a shift in attitude, you will be able to join in. This is the time not only for imagination, but for *courage;* your life isn't at stake, but the quality of it may be!

TRY, TRY AGAIN? ARE YOU SERIOUS?

The old adage, "If at first you don't succeed, try, try again," is good advice, but it is even better when a crucial phrase is added: "*each time, a different way.*" It's a life-fulfilling philosophy of trying out hunches and getting past the obvious first thought that builds both confidence and skill.

Start learning these life skills while you are in college. Begin building relationships with campus professors, counselors, and staff now and with employers you meet through internships and jobs. Watch how others act and experiment with ways to present yourself; communicate with more experienced people, take their tips, and progress in valuable relationships that may continue. You will discover intriguing ideas and find fascinating careers you didn't know anything about.

If you join the campus newspaper, ask alumni who are journalists to come speak to your staff. Invite great editors of newspapers to critique an issue or ask its marketing director for ideas to promote your paper. Get yourself a minute on the radio station to itemize the news or opinions you write. Read other college newspapers and write a fan letter to another fine reporter; you might make a friend you could not otherwise meet. Don't deny yourself these experiences. They offer you a safe harbor for experimentation; you can't get fired if you fail in these experiments, but you can be introduced to something or someone new if you try. These are life-affirming success skills.

Don't settle for a boring grade-oriented college life. Don't turn college into a test. You'll end up merely passing: passing tests, passing time, passing up possibilities for achievement, passing through life. You'll end up living a life that others expect instead of finding one exactly suited for yourself. Avoid the "good student" trap. Yes, it requires real courage to develop your own character and interests. Make college an ongoing experiment to find out what you like to study, how you actually learn, and what you would like to do with your major.

BECOMING AN ACHIEVER BY BUILDING A NETWORK

Here are some specific ways you can put the ideas in this chapter into practice. Reframe your way of thinking. Don't be afraid to seek out and connect with accomplished people—other students, professors, and employers. Remember, this is the first step in taking yourself seriously and building self-worth. Give up trying to secure your place in the world only by obediently fulfilling other people's expectations. Again, don't be passive! First, you need to find out what other people know. Second, find out where you want to forge ahead and make your unique contribution. Think of yourself as both a builder and an explorer in the process of discovery. Part of what you have to discover is how to interact with other people. There are several ways that you can begin this process—join or start a study group, participate in campus activities, and be people-friendly.

Join or Start a Study Group

If you can't find a study group meeting regularly, start one. Invite some classmates over for pizza to brainstorm about how to study together or to collaborate on a project. You will learn the following:

- How to organize and prepare material for your classes and set appropriate deadlines to avoid procrastinating
- How to divide the work among a group according to everyone's interests
- How to exchange assignments so you get a chance to try everything
- How to build friendships with some of the other students in your study group

Investigate the courses that excite you. There are bound to be many that beckon to you from your college catalog. Find what you like about a course instead of finding a reason not to like it. Allow yourself to become interested in and pursue those courses. Write papers in appropriate fields and subjects, *even if they do not appear on the professors' lists*. Talk to your professors about the ideas that excite you. They hope you will. You can even look in the alumni directory from the alumni office to find graduates who are employed in fields that interest you. Go meet them. (More on this point in chapter 2.)

Take the minimal risk of asking questions of your academic advisor, professors, instructors, and administrators. They expect you to do this. They will think more of you, not less, and they will help with more than just answers. Ask them to share the following:

- How they got started
- Surprises they found along the way
- Trends they recognize
- Advice on your best academic or career bets
- Names of people, organizations, and books that can guide you
- Course and career recommendations

Check Out and Join Campus Activities That Appeal to You

Get a list of activities from the student affairs office. Pick the activities that appeal to you most, from a campus radio station to the newspaper, from drama to debate to soccer, from student government to the glee club to the business club. Then do more than just join. Get *involved*. Make your involvement an exploration of your abilities. Sit in on a few meetings and events so you can pick activities that excite you, whether you have experience with them or not. Then, volunteer in a higher, more visible role—one that you haven't tried before. Your willingness will make you valuable to the group.

Make new friends from class and clubs. Introduce yourself, no matter how hard it is at first. Someone has to speak first or else no one will; you can all just there sit silent and isolated. But how do you start? I've

Make Yourself People-Friendly

If you sat next to someone you did not know and he or she started a conversation, would you find it unwelcome? Of course not. So, why not start one yourself? With that as a cue, start changing your behavior. Today, sit next to someone and introduce yourself. Ask a few polite questions. Learn to be curious; it will open possibilities. The other person is very unlikely to think less of you or that you are strange. Get over passively waiting for others to discover you. Be the explorer—it's exactly what most successful people do in real life. Start practicing now. This change in behavior only has an upside!

observed thousands of times how students enter a large lecture hall. It doesn't matter whether it's a small, rural liberal arts campus or a large urban hall in the middle of a big city. Each one of the 70 or 700 students sits spread far apart from the rest. The first students who enter choose seats in the back. Then incoming peers pick seats midway back, on the sides, or in the middle. They act like magnets, repelling each other.

I have watched this from the stage where I'm going to give a lecture on success. I start my talk asking about the students' choices of seats. I ask them to count each empty seat between themselves and their classmates as a single unit of fear—doubling that number for empty rows between them and the lecturer at the front of class. It's fear of each other that keeps us apart. One hallmark of successful people is that they take steps to plow through that fear and build courage. You can start that process in the first lecture you attend!

You can probably guess what I do next: I ask everyone to move down, sit beside each other, and introduce themselves. Of course, no one wants to do it, so I have to ask a second time. Everyone is reluctant even then, but most of them do it. And the energy in the room immediately changes. The chance that people will become friends, colleagues, business partners, or even marriage partners dramatically increases! My lecture begins to take on a deeper meaning because everyone already has begun to practice one of the success skills: taking the risk of connecting with others. It takes courage. Try this yourself, even if it is really difficult for you. Shyness gets you nothing, but persistence gets you everything.

You will have created a fine opportunity. After all, meeting someone at a lecture is much easier than introducing yourself at a dance, another one of those tough encounters. Each one of us is hoping that someone else will come over to us. Since we're all waiting, it might as well be you who starts the ball rolling. In high school, usually everyone knew each other. But colleges are typically so much bigger. Perhaps even more importantly, people need to know each other, whether they live off campus or in dorms. To start, just smile; that's the human cue that "we're in this together." Introduce yourself to several people. Remember their names and their interests—even considering jotting these things down in your notebook or on your computer. Suggest meeting for lunch. Then, invite a few to join you at events and lectures. Keep building friendships, introducing one group to another. Later in life, they will become your first network of support. Remember, everyone is waiting for you to start.

There is a vitality, a life force, an energy, a quickening that is translated through you into action. And because there is only one of you in all time, this expression is unique. And if you block it, it will never exist through any other medium, and be lost. The world will not have it. It is not your business to determine how good it is, nor how valuable, nor how it compares with other expressions. It is your business to keep it yours clearly and directly, to keep the channel open.
—Martha Graham

Caroline's Story: Finding Yourself in College

Caroline had been programmed for health care work by her family, who wanted a stable career for her. She was disciplined and determined in college, but she was disappointed in her classes. She didn't even like them. After her junior year, she nearly had a breakdown. When she looked at what she really cared about, it seemed like something too trivial for her and her family to accept: she loved making jewelry. This was certainly not the higher calling for healing that her family had in mind for her; yet she was enthusiastic about this hobby, which had become her part-time livelihood. She had earned her way in college by stringing beads for necklaces and bracelets and selling them to friends, at flea markets, even to boutiques. Realizing that she had no background to push this to a career, Caroline switched her major to business to learn about marketing and took courses in design to learn more about color and pattern. She also wrote a history paper on the promotional campaign of a major jewelry line. Discovering her own real values, standing up to her family for herself, and taking her interests seriously enough to pursue them led her to find college courses that were inspiring rather than dispiriting. She came *home* to her studies and to herself. Like her, you can use college to discover your talents and build on them to create passionate interests and ways to explore them.

Summary: Words to Remember

Behavior to Avoid	Behavior to Embrace
• "Good student" behavior	• Imaginativeness
• Obedience	• Friendliness
• Passivity	• Curiosity
• Settling	• Expecting more
• Shyness	• Courage
• Fear	• Risk-taking
• Lack of involvement	• Network-building

Chapter 2
Building Relationships
from Friends to Mentors

Our chief want in life is somebody who shall make us do what we can.
— *Ralph Waldo Emerson*

At the age of thirty-four, a returning student signed up for a senior American history class and, for the first time, found himself enthralled by his professor. He found it unusually easy to stay after class to talk about the reading assignments and interpretations of what he had previously thought of as facts. He could hardly restrain himself from complimenting the professor who brought the subject to life; his professor, impressed and interested, encouraged him to enroll in graduate school. In June, immediately after he graduated, he wrote his appreciation not in a thank you card but in a Father's Day card. A Father's Day card when there were fewer than ten years between them? Yes, a strong mentorship had developed that most students can only hope for. As for the professor, you can bet he never had to search through his files to remember for which student he was writing letters of recommendation. But what made the student so special? He was not the most brilliant student. There can be only one "most" brilliant student, after all. What can the rest of us do to develop such a bond with our professors? Become interested in the subject and in them. There is nothing like profound expressed interest on which to build a relationship.

Yet relationships are tricky things, no matter how much we need them. No getting around that. The dynamics of hope, love, happiness, and betrayal between friends and lovers have long been the subject of books, songs, and movies. But the relationship between student and pro-fessor is a unique one, not much written about, that you will encounter every day in college. That special relationship is just what college offers you—a chance to have professors transform your life. But it is different from anything you have known before, because it is complicated by its complete inequality in power.

BEING A PROTÉGÉ

In every course you take, you spend hours with professors who could change your life. Learn to relate to them even if you aren't sure how. Your sincerity and politeness alone will make a good impression. If you look around your class or seminar, you will probably see a range of behaviors, from passive to rebellious, exhibited by students who haven't yet begun to distinguish their teachers from their parents.

Think of yourself as the apprentice or *protégé* to your professor, who could be your mentor. This model is closer to what a productive college relationship should be. In the preindustrial, precollege age, young apprentices began as indentured servants to master artists or craftsmen in order to learn their trades. Performing menial tasks at first, apprentices gradually learned to develop their skills to a master level. Only then were they able to take over or to strike out on their own. The same kind of sys-tem, ancient but still valuable, is embedded in higher education. If you think of your professors in the role of master and play the part of appren-tice (without the indentured servant part!), then you can then identify what you would like to learn and reap the rewards awaiting you.

> *Other people can't make you see with their eyes. At best, they can encourage you to use your own.*
> —*Aldous Huxley*

Building Relationships with Professors

In high school, teachers routinely notified you when your work was either overdue or unsatisfactory. Not so in college; now it's up to you. Don't make the mistake of relating to your professors the way you did to your teachers. Ask for their advice. Inquire about their other courses. Once you find profes-sors whom you respect, it's up to you to initiate the relationship. The best way is to visit during office hours and talk to them. Ask about their own stories or experiences, or for advice on a specific problem, or to elaborate on something they said in class. They expect you to visit and talk; it shows that you are committed to learning.

When you find professors you really admire, take as many courses as possible from them. Get the scoop from classmates you trust about which professors are excellent. It's expected of all great students to take the initiative and enroll in their classes. Why not? You are investing years of time and thousands of dollars—do your part. Read a few of their more accessible published papers and books and ask them about what they've written. Talk informally with your professors after class about their lives and research and share yours. If you express interest, the professors will regard you as a serious student.

In short, demonstrate your curiosity. Your professors will not only understand it, but also appreciate it. Only then can they begin coaching you. Don't worry about being seen as an apple polisher or as a student who is buttering them up for a better grade; they can spot this a mile away. You are seriously building your first network of value!

Many successful executives, artists, and other have told me how critical mentors were to them when they were in college and then later in their careers. Mentors encouraged their personal and professional development by offering advice and leads, encouraging them through difficult periods, and motivating them to continue to push ahead. Even more important, their mentors helped identify strong talents and encouraged their development. Behind successful people often are mentors who encourge them to pursue particular careers and open doors of opportunity that they might not see. Mentors connect them with prospective employers, help them get into graduate school, and lend perspective and guidance later in their careers.

Follow their lead. Turn professors into your mentors and learn how to build on what you have learned and to apply it constructively. Or, you could sit in class and passively take notes, which amounts to having a sign on your forehead that says, "Ignore me. Pass on any opportunities to someone else."

A highly acclaimed computer analyst told me that his career actually had been formed because of one charismatic and brilliant professor. As a student, he was clearly awed, coming to class early and staying late to discuss the problems he had been working on. During that year, the professor encouraged him to change his major from industrial engineering to economics and introduced him to a prominent professor, who offered him a fellowship for advanced study. It is not likely that he could have done this on his own. Other students thought he was singled out because he was lucky as well as talented. It's easy to label that as luck, but it is certainly neither the only, nor the most important, factor. After all, there are thousands of talented students all around you. This student was chosen because he put in effort to do the choosing himself.

In the same way, a well-known placement specialist in the field of industrial design was aided in her design studies and her behavioral skills by the only woman on the faculty at that college. The professor, who later became a role model for many other female students, knew how difficult it would be for young women to be accepted in the business world and mentored the aspiring executive with business ideas and social skills. She met with her student over long lunches and gave help and advice on strategies, etiquette, and social interaction for more than a decade after the student had graduated. The former student has become a highly respected businesswoman thanks to the encouragement of her knowledgeable, caring mentor.

SIGNIFICANT OTHERS

Professors are not the only people on campus whose friendship you'll be grateful for. Your advisors, department heads, and their staff are also knowledgeable and helpful. Administrative staffers are responsible for student activities, records, and grants, and they can be tremendously helpful to you in even more ways than your professors, whose expertise is usually confined to their areas of study. Another tip: speakers who are invited to lecture on campus are often receptive to being approached by you after their lectures, and they may expect you to follow up later with a letter that states "We met at...."

If you need encouragement or advice (and who doesn't?), the student activities staff provides miracles every day. If you need special permission to take a course not usually open to you or if you need to petition to receive credit for a past course, your best bets lie with administrators. They should know the rules of the game, however much it changes, and can show you the best way to present yourself. If you need financial aid, fellowships, grants, or work-study, go to the financial aid staff. That's their job, and they chose it because they like helping students. They welcome your requests for help with a problem they can solve.

Think of administrators, counselors, and professionals as friends who are there to help you. Many will provide assistance when you really need it. They can change the course of your life, but only if you ask them. If you approach someone who can't help, find someone else who will.

You may encounter conflicts about your choice of major or intended career path with your own family, particularly your parents. This can require very delicate negotiation. Sometimes you can come to terms with them, sometimes not. When you can't make a decision between your desires and those of your parents, testing may be helpful for negotiation. You can take a battery of psychological, ability, and vocational tests to demonstrate your strengths, confirm your choice to yourself, and help persuade your family. Sometimes it is advisable to fulfill both agendas by taking a double major. Opposing your parents can be expensive if it comes down to having to pay for your education yourself, but it is worth the investment. Don't try this alone; talk to a psychologist or career counselor.

Strategies for Cultivating Mentors

It's up to you to get to know your professors. Don't expect them to discover your talents immediately and point you in the right direction. They won't; they can't. They have so many students. Therefore, they can only notice you and help you if you reveal yourself. They are not mind readers, so you need to engage with them in open-ended discussions during office hours or after class. It is then that you can ask if there is a chance for you to be a research associate, attend professional meetings, and/or help with any tasks in return for the chance to associate with significant people in your field—even if you are not paid! Working for no pay is better than not working at all. It provides experience, and it is as valuable as the classroom work that you pay for. In these ways, you learn how to link to ideas and people who might, in turn, help and inspire you.

How do you begin? Visit your professor during office hours and ask if you can help research one of their own projects. This may sound intimidating, but you might be surprised—professors rarely have adequate staff and can always use the extra help. By getting involved in part of a large project, you will find out more about the world of research. You might find that an area of the subject is compelling. You might find a topic for a paper of your own. Don't be afraid to ask for suggestions on how you can find your way. Occasionally, something will happen that you wouldn't have planned on. The very act of discussing your interests and your work begins the mentor-protégé relationship, which will reward you in powerful ways you can't even guess. By practicing your research, analysis, interviewing, and organization skills with guidance, you will develop interests and experience that could make or change a major or a career.

Every successful person whom I have interviewed admitted that they were the apple of someone else's eye. They were inspired to be bold, to take themselves seriously, and to go for their dreams. They did it because someone they admired believed they could.

Mentoring Success Stories

Frank Gehry, the world-renowned architect of Disney Hall, did not think of studying architecture in college. Following in his brother's footsteps by majoring in chemical engineering, he worked with a professor to develop glaze fittings, which seemed to suit him. After he got to know the professor, that professor suggested a new direction of study where Gehry could sparkle—architecture. If this professor had not seen Gehry's talent and interest and matched it to a more appropriate major, he may not have found his dream career. As Gehry transformed from an average student to an excellent one, he began hanging out with professors he admired. He became included in "everything from working on projects to dinners at their houses," while most other students were merely into fraternities. The dean, who became his mentor, recommended him for a job with Victor Gruen, a new, progressive, and unusually idealistic firm, and later helped him get paid to write a thesis, which actually led Gehry to develop a Mexican town. His mentor then recommended him to Harvard in the field of urban planning. He continued to build relationships as well as create uniquely inspired architecture. I encourage you to read more about him, because his career started in college with one professor's guidance.

Gloria Steinem, feminist, founder of Ms. Magazine, and cofounder of the National Organization for Women, went to Smith College. There she found a professor of Indian history whom she could talk to. She did not think of her as a mentor, just an understanding professor. Near her graduation in 1956, she was faced with what her mentor labeled as two "dead-end" jobs: the first was researching for Time/Life (which, at that time, did not allow women to write), and the second was getting engaged to be married. Her mentor suggested that she turn these offers down and, instead, go to India on an experimental internship. This was the first of what turned out to be three such fellowships that transformed her life. It inspired a larger mission than she ever would have imagined. Awakened politically, she began her career as a writer and activist. Her life story might encourage you, too, to take risks recommended by your professors. They are risks because their outcomes cannot be predicted. The only thing that is known is that once you embark on a new journey, you are suddenly open to new ideas and experiences. Once you develop an openness to new ideas and experiences, and you learn to trust the risk-taking process, which is not clearly defined, these choices will allow you to grow throughout your life. But know that you do not act alone; you need the encouragement and direction of trusted professors and guides.

It may be difficult to admit that you crave this unique mentor-protégé relationship and even harder to think of why any professor would want to invest time in you. Please realize that such relationships are actually mutually beneficial. If you believe that you are just imposing on a professor's valuable time, you'll make it harder for yourself. Actually, it works in just the opposite way: you will be, to a great extent, helping both of you. You need mentors, and professors need protégés like you. Although many professors live largely in a theoretical world of research, and some of them would rather do research than anything else, they can still receive great gratification through feedback from talented and committed students.

Although you might never know it, a professor's world is partly political, and many find that aspect distasteful. Their academic career is based on publishing, getting grants, and serving on academic committees and university associations. They also have many administrative duties within their department. These tasks are time-consuming and usually obligatory. Who, then, provides the necessary positive feedback and assistance that professors need to carry on? You can do that, as a vitally interested, gifted, and willing student.

Having written about her own difficult early life, novelist Carolyn See found college to be "her only real home." In her modern American literature seminar, she found her mentor in Professor John Espey. She signed up for all his courses, worked as his teaching assistant, became his first doctoral candidate, got a Woodrow Wilson teaching fellowship through his recommendation, and ultimately married him. She continued to write novels, even a few with him and with their daughter.

Mollie Gregory, author of *Women Who Run the Show*, began her screenwriting career in college. The chair of her department recommended her for the MCA Script Award. That, in turn, led to four more national awards, an internship, and graduate school. Her success in college became the catalyst for her life devoted to film.

Do not be afraid of overstepping your role as student. Do not remain silent. Keep in mind that professors love being able to shape students' lives. This is why they chose to teach in the first place. By recognizing that the student-professor relationship is reciprocal, you will be able to give more, and your professors will give more to you in return.

Annette's Story: A Professor Intervenes

Sometimes professors can help even with seemingly insurmountable personal problems, as the following story shows.

Annette was studying art history when a family problem arose that would have cost her an entire college education, had it not been for the intervention of one of her professors. When Annette's father fell ill and lost his job, her family was unable to make its mortgage payments, let alone meet Annette's tuition. Panicked, Annette was considering quitting to find a full-time job in order to support her family. Her favorite art professor convinced her to stay on by helping her get a 50% scholarship and a part-time job at night as a guard. The job, which allowed her some time to study, was a perfect arrangement. The continuous moral support that her professor provided was also vital to Annette's college career, which turned out to be extraordinary, including honors, grants, and two articles coauthored with her mentor.

Claude's Story: Learning the Dynamics

This story is a best-case scenario illustrating the rewards that can come from building a mentor relationship with a professor.

Claude, a graduate student in sociology, became a research assistant to a prominent grant-funded professor at a major state university. While assigned to what seemed like a relatively insignificant task in one area of data collection, Claude saw where he might contribute more than the job required: he could coordinate the schedules and chart the progress of the other data-collecting student researchers. By developing a specialized role for himself, Claude soon became indispensable. Furthermore, he enrolled in all of the professor's courses over the following several years so he could continue learning more about the professor's theories and continue working for him. Claude made it part of his day to stop casually by his professor's office to chat about assignments and research, as well as daily life.

For his efforts, Claude got even more in return. His rewards lay not just in raises and a full scholarship, though they were tremendously helpful. He was also given a part of his professor's project to work on. This included a grant to support himself and a topic for his thesis, which in turn led to an impressive doctoral program. In addition to getting a scholarship and a research project, he had the valuable opportunity to watch a successful professor at work. Claude observed his professor in the process of writing and obtaining grants, implementing a major research program, and becoming involved in reciprocal relationships with other professionals at that university and across the country. He was also privy to the politically savvy way the professor acted in his committee assignments on tenure and development and got a unique chance to witness the professor's style of decision-making and team-play. When Claude himself was ready to apply for a doctoral program, his mentor personally referred him to a team of prominent professors who had a multitude of connections to offer. The sponsorship of Claude's first professor was the catapult to Claude's progress in his field. No student who merely earned straight As, as laudatory as that is, could have gained so much.

Do you think that what Claude did to get his initial job was worth the risk? What risk? He took the chance of being snubbed by some cynics in his class, but he succeeded far beyond any of his disdaining peers. Their self-righteous refusal to "use" their professors diminished their opportunities in their professional lives. At the end of the term, some of the bright but not connected students did have good grades—but here's what they *didn't* have: references, exposure to new people who could open doors, and new insights beyond what their conscientious study could offer. The cynical students were hurt by their beliefs that school is only for passing tests and racking up grades. Ultimately, *they* are the ones who misuse the system when they fail to recognize their part in this human enterprise of higher education.

Why do these things? The answer is simple: to develop the essential skill of taking risks to link yourself to real activities done by real people working in their fields. Only after connecting in this way can you begin to find out what compels you. You cannot choose in a vacuum. Besides, the more active you are, the more you'll learn about and develop your authentic self.

WHAT YOU CAN DO

Start taking the risk of forming relationships with one or more of your professors. At first it is likely to feel uncomfortable or even frightening, but that is true for all new and worthwhile pursuits. In actuality, the risk is minimal compared to the potential rewards. Be fair to yourself; you are not stupid, or you wouldn't be in college in the first place. You're in school because you want to learn more. Start by confronting your own fears. For example, if you find that you do not understand the whole subject or any part of it, don't hide. Go talk to your professor and tell him or her that you are having trouble. Don't be afraid of being vulnerable. If your professor is really good, he or she will pinpoint your difficulty and find another way to explain the concepts that elude you. All it takes is your ability to open up and overcome your fear. If you don't, you will fall behind and sink into thinking that you are stupid. If your professor doesn't help you, get involved in a study group of your peers, or find a tutor. One of the traits that separates those who are stuck from the achievers is that while others let fear stop them, achievers don't give up, even when they are afraid. Mark Twain said it best: "Courage is not the absence of fear, but the mastery of it."

A word of caution is necessary here. Too much of a good thing is not always better. Turning a professor into a god who has all the answers is neither healthy nor productive. It violates a basic ethical code and precludes any meaningful exchange of ideas. The same goes for turning your professor into a lover. Attaching yourself to professor-mentors you respect for their intelligence and knowledge is not the same as hero worship or infatuation. It is possible that you will become entranced by a seemingly ideal professor. If this happens, know that it is a typical reaction, a phase to be lived through. If it gets dicey and you are upset or feel threatened, speak in confidence to a counselor on campus—use the free services. Like the apprentice, as you develop your expertise, you will eventually stand next to your professor as an equal. These are natural phases of growth from which we shouldn't shy away.

You can begin the process of establishing relationships with professors and turning one or two of them into real first mentors in college. It's up to you to approach them and get them started. Relax—you don't need exciting stories to tell, and you don't need to speak only about yourself. Instead, ask professors about the new findings in their field, what they are encountering in class, how they became involved in their field, or if they had to do it all over again, what discipline they would choose. Listen to what they say, and follow up with another question. Don't wait for them to pause so that you can tell them a story. Develop the art of conversation by interviewing and really listening to a story. Then, remember their advice and their stories and talk to them again, following up by talking about your progress.

Turning your professor into a mentor requires the following:

1.   You admire the professor and are interested in the subject matter.
2.   You ask questions in class and during office hours and follow up with ideas.

3.   You build rapport by reporting back, asking for further leads, sharing what you have discovered, and asking your professor's advice.

4.   You ask for help if the assignment is harder than those you are used to.

5.   You find ways to complete your requirements, not just give excuses.

6.   You are appreciative, show gratitude, and work without complaining.

RETURNING STUDENTS

Even though the average college student is now over twenty-four years old, most students still think that eighteen is the "correct" age for starting college. Once a small percentage of the student body, older students are now the norm. But if you are an older student, you may feel alienated, as if you don't fit into college life. To correct that view, think of two ends of a scale: one end is labeled feeling, the other reality. They are hardly ever congruent. What you *feel* is not usually what is going on. If you can make a clear distinction between your feelings and the objective situation, you are less likely to think you don't belong. What is the real risk of being a few years older than some of the others? The answer: None.

A caution: finding a professor who is willing to become a mentor is sometimes more difficult for older, so-called "nontraditional" students. If you are a lot older than the traditional college age, being the same age as your professor can be initially uncomfortable for both of you. Returning students often make one of two basic errors: overplaying their role (reminding professors that they have life experience) or, more frequently, underplaying it (playing dumb). While returning students might feel they should be more equal in status to the faculty, they are still dependent on advice and guidance. So in many ways they are equivalent to the traditional student and should not lead with a sense of their greater maturity. On the other hand, if you are a returning student, you should not make the mistake, out of fear of failing, of falling back into a completely subservient student role. It is easy to regress from your actual age of thirty or forty to become, in effect, an anxious adolescent, reverting to the emotional age you were when you were last in school. These errors are easy to fall into, but they are still a costly mistake. Accept your student status, but preserve your mature adult self.

Much like divorced people starting to date again at forty, returning students suddenly find themselves with the same fears they had when they were eighteen. Being aware of this phenomenon may soothe your awkwardness and anxiety, but it is still somewhat difficult. Most return-ing students, as well as traditional students, experience strange and unex-pected mood swings, whose cause may be a mystery to you. If you deny the anxiety you feel, you may be tempted to prove your worth and impress your professors with your own worldliness and prior successful experiences. You could unintentionally be creating an unhelpful, com-petitive situation. Relax; you'll find that you are a far better student than you ever expected to be.

Roberta's Story: Back to School

The following story shows some of the perils peculiar to older students returning to school.

At thirty-eight, Roberta had come back to school to study psychol-ogy at the graduate level after several years of administrative work at a mental health clinic. Her most difficult adjustment to school was her offense at some of the simplistic ideas her professors presented to students who had never seen a real mental health environment. While her pro-fessor had theoretical research on his side, he had never run such a clinic. Roberta wanted to hold forth in a debate to show her great practical experience. Instead, she had to learn to let go of her need to prove her-self right or superior. She had to find an appropriate balance in which she could bring her own experience to class yet still show her respect for her professor. To her surprise, she had to master a new diplomacy. Had she not, she would have broadcast the message: "I know more about this sub-ject than you do. I am just taking this course because it's required. But I resent your not teaching me anything new."

How else could Roberta have used and even benefited from her past work experience? She might have invited feedback on problems with which the mental health clinic staff struggled. Or she could have related some of her practical experiences as an administrator working with psy-chologists and psychiatrists. She could reveal some of their successes and failures with different kinds of patients. Or, she might even have sug-gested a pilot research program to train administrators to be counselors.

THE ORIGINAL NETWORK:
WHEN YOU AND YOUR FAMILY DISAGREE

It may help to keep in mind that friction between parents' expectations and their children's choices is legendary—no matter the age of the children! It's been going on for thousands of years. Just read the many biographies of artists pursuing their passionate careers against their parents' objections. Composer Robert Schumann yearned to compose music but found himself at war with his parents, who wanted him go into law, a stable and respectable profession. Oral historian Studs Terkel went to law school to pacify his parents but returned to his first love, interviewing jazz musicians on radio and recording oral histories of working people. There are many such stories; yours might be one. If it is, read biographies to understand the agony they went through and choices that each made to be true to themselves and to honor their families when they could.

But sometimes an opposite emotion takes hold: the desire to escape from your family. Most people have, at different times in their lives, wished for different families, perhaps ones that were more successful and well connected or more encouraging and supportive, whether financially, intellectually, or socially. It can be so hard to accept advice from those you want to separate from that often you may refuse to talk to them or even use their networks to explore leads about educational opportunities and careers. You may flatly turn them down, believing that you can do better—or at least differently—on our own. Of course, you might, but you give up a lot by overlooking these sources. Why not take the advantage of what is offered?

Your family experience is usually very different from families on TV sitcoms. There's a good possibility that your parents have experienced hardship themselves; they might be divorced, downsized at work, or surviving as immigrants. They are as anxious about their own future careers as they are about yours. They may insist that your major be entirely practical and lead directly to a secure career, but your ideas may be very different.

All growth requires change. To change, you have to let go of part of what you know, but you can't forget everything or turn into a completely different person. You have to maintain your grounding in your character but, at the same time, allow yourself to be open to new challenges. Therefore, stay in contact with family and friends. Keep some photos. Plan to see them on holidays. But you don't have to build your future life in college around them. Make new friends. Turn to professors, advisors, and counselors for new ideas, even in times when you are unhappy. College is an essential part of separating from your parents and becoming your own person.

First-Generation Challenges

Many of you are the first in your family to attend college. As first-generation students, you might find that your parents cannot give relevant real-world advice and sometimes are even off the mark about what college should provide. When that happens, you have to find the most appropriate advice and follow it. That often means educating your parents, which may be the furthest thing from your own agenda. Sometimes they hold to their own vision. If you are a first-generation American, remember that your parents' very stubbornness has strength behind it; it led them to a new country. They are coping with a different language and culture as well as the responsibility of raising you. The phrase "rendering unto Caesar his due" translates well for just this kind of dilemma. In this context, it means learning the high skill of satisfying authority's demands while at the same time satisfying your own needs. It's not easy, but it's possible.

DISTANCE LEARNING: THE VIRTUAL MENTORSHIP

"Distance learning" is an inevitable revolution in higher education. It makes use of computers and the Internet and offers a different kind of interactive study. It allows you to interact effectively with your professors despite their being separated in space from you.

Who Participates?

Most effective for a highly motivated student, distance learning provides a way to take a myriad of courses, and even full programs, via the computer. While you never have to physically come to class, you do have to be focused to learn on your own and take assignments solo or with other students whom you may meet only online. Many traditional students take classes online that are not offered during the regular on-campus schedule. The greatest appeal, however, is if you are an adult student with constraints of distance and time. You may work full-time and have a family to support, but you are also dedicated to advancing your careers. Electronic access to learning resources, plus the award of a legitimate credential, will confirm your ambition and your choice.

Is It Comparable?

Accredited, established distance learning can offer the same caliber of instruction as traditional college classes. More and more, it offers full curricula and awards undergraduate and graduate degrees. Some colleges are forming new alliances and consortia with multiple universities to build and offer an extensive list of courses and programs.

Is It Easier?

Don't be fooled into thinking a distance learning class is going to be easier, faster, or shorter. Many students who do well online admit that it requires far more time than they thought. So rather than a quick-and-easy course, it may take more time, including weekends, to do all the work of reading texts, watching videos, writing papers, and communicating via e-mail. It requires an ability to work independently, because there is no live professor there to remind you to do your assignments. You can join study groups online and e-mail your professors. Distance learning requires you to manage your time, connections, and concentration.

> ## Questions to Ask Yourself in Every Course You Take
>
> 1. *What part of this course truly interests me?*
> 2. *What more do I want to know?*
> 3. *What can I ask my professors during office hours to help me learn more?*
> 4. *How can I learn to improve my work—my papers and exams?*
> 5. *How can I use my assignments, papers, or projects to my advantage?*
> 6. *Who can guide me in pursuing this course?*
> 7. *What careers relate to this study?*

How Will I Connect with My Professor?

The most difficult aspect is that you will have to learn to interact differently with professors, since there is no personal contact, no easy way to chat during or after class, and no communicaton during office hours. It is entirely up to you to ask your professors for clarification, help, and advice—and be patient while waiting for a reply. Instead of a person with a fixed schedule, your professor will become more of a facilitator to help you learn. If you need support, you can tap into a peer network comprised of other students from a variety of social, cultural, economic, and experiential backgrounds. If you find that you are enthusiastic and interested in the subject, you might look up your professor's publications and awards and continue your studies with more courses from him or her. You may have to become an active fan and supporter, making known your similar interests, thus overcoming the absence of in-person contact. Upper-class and graduate students have the best chance of building a rapport that leads to a mentor-protégé relationship.

All successful alumni report that the more you are engaged in university life, the richer your experiences and relationships will be. Why not start now?

FREQUENTLY ASKED QUESTIONS

Q. I'm overworked, overwhelmed, and stressed out. What can I do?

A. First, a little dose of reality: Yes, going to college offers many opportunities and demands much in return. Yes, it's harder than it looks. There are deadlines, papers, exams, requirements. Yes, you're being tested and evaluated. Yes, you may be involved in clubs and/or have to work part time, too. Yes, there's little room for rest and relaxation without compromising something. Yes, you're tired and probably broke most of the time. And yes, sometimes stress is a motivator to get everything done as well as you can.

Still, you can manage your time better. Map out all your requirements and then make a time chart of what you have to do. Focus on one project at a time rather than getting blown away by the enormity of it all. Find some pleasure—meet with friends for an hour, go to a movie, dance. But don't squander time. Every one of us gets twenty-four hours in each day; it's up to us to schedule it well.

Q. I am quite depressed. Am I alone?

A. No, a great many people feel depressed briefly or for the long term. Many have written about how they dealt with their own bouts of dark depression or disability: psychiatrists Sigmund Freud and Kay Jamison; journalists Jane Pauley, Art Buchwald, and Andrew Solomon; Olympic winner Greg Louganis. All of them describe their feelings and how they got help so that they could become more alive and understanding. You can too. Start with a visit to one of your campus's psychologists or counselors—they are there to help you.

Q. I have received totally bad advice from my academic advisor and my professor and will have to take another course to make up a lost credit in order to graduate. Now I'm dealing with an idiotic financial aid officer who won't give me a better loan. Should I write a letter to the president and tell him how ineffective his college really is or what? Who do I complain to?

A. Don't waste your time complaining. Yes, you were right to ask for advice in the first place. You may encounter misinformation, but you still have to deal with it the best you can. See if you have misrepresented your records. Take your transcripts, along with the advice you have been given, to another person—perhaps the vice president of undergraduate studies—to find out what else you need to qualify or to ask for reconsideration. In addition, check online for better loans, and ask your classmates for leads. Learning how to accept responsibility for yourself in a positive way is a key to your own success, and not only in college.

KEYS TO A SUCCESSFUL TRANSITION

Attitude Test

Check out your attitudes, both positive and negative. If you're doing all you can, congratulate yourself. If you can see where and how

---

Active Plans to Follow for Success

- *Your classes are prime places to meet friends for life. Smile and introduce yourself, especially at the beginning of classes. Show your interest by asking how fellow students are doing; invite them to lunch or to join you in a class or campus event.*
- *For career leads, join clubs and organizations based on your own interests or your major.*
- *To meet people and develop friendships, get involved in support groups, study groups, or one of the special programs, such as the "first-year experience" programs, gaining popularity on many campuses.*

---

you're not using college to help you learn more and boost your ability and confidence, then start to change for the better. If you don't know how, ask a professor or counselor to help. They can and will. Remember why you're here!

If any of the following describe you, then it is time to change your ways:

- I'm usually late to class.
- I procrastinate much of the time.
- I sit in the back of every class.
- I've slept in class more than twice.
- I don't talk to classmates or professors.
- I party too much.
- I often have a hangover.
- I see cramming as a way of life.
- I haven't scheduled enough study time (less than one hour per unit per week).
- I've been turning in sloppy papers.
- I've failed pop quizzes more than twice.
- I'm tired all the time.
- I feel inadequate most of the time.

- I'm taking too few units each semester/quarter.
- I often eat solo.

But knowing your problems and doing something about it are miles apart. You can't do change through intention or affirmations only. Get smart. Get help from a counselor and/or professor in order to redirect yourself. Make college a successful place for you to learn—not just to endure or even escape from.

Especially for first-year students, it is normal to get overwhelmed by so much newness and by the inevitable emotional roller coasters. Lack of comfort makes you edgy, sometimes depressed. You will see the tell-tale signs: you may gain weight, oversleep, doze through classes, and even develop somewhat weird phobias. But you can better resolve these problems once you own up to them. Even if you don't feel like it, open yourself up to valuable resources, such as professors, counselors, and friends. Don't backpedal. Don't stay isolated. Don't quit!

Tips for Surviving College

- Know that, while friends are essential, it is a natural process to change many friends as you advance. But you will keep a few others all your life.
- Learn to be a better friend yourself. Listen and remember as well as talk.
- Practice developing social skills, as well as academic skills.
- Remember, you are learning to be more independent. But all growing is hard, even growing up.
- Be willing, not afraid or embarrassed, to ask for help. Getting tutored, counseled, or advised is expected. In fact, your student fees pay for just this kind of help.
- Some periods are tougher than others. Count on having feelings of anxiety or depression, loneliness, and isolation. Some periods are tougher than others, but these feelings should pass. Don't act out on them by dropping out or doing anything harmful. Definitely ask for help if you feel down for longer than two weeks.
- See your academic advisor each semester to make sure you are on the right track. Check out the advice of other professors, too.
- Look for campus newspaper listings and posters announcing special lectures by prominent experts. Ask questions, learn, and make friends with others interested in the subjects.

- Make yourself join clubs or activities. Get the full list, usually available online or in the student union.
- Don't be overwhelmed by your professors. Learn to ask questions and speak up in class and during office hours. Professors expect you to.
- Read your college catalog, and note required classes as well as ones that simply appeal to you. Look for ratings and opinions on the professors who teach them; find the best professors and take their classes.
- Keep your own personal and permanent college file of courses, credits, grade reports, transcripts, letters of recommendation, lists of activities, and résumé in a portfolio or plastic box. Be sure to label and keep a master copy of everything; make copies when necessary.

Competition also makes you anxious. While you might have been a star in high school—perhaps first in your class, valedictorian, or most popular—you start from scratch in college. You will meet many of your classmates who also were stars in their high schools. Don't think of competing; instead, rejoice, join in, and participate cooperatively. Be friendly. Look for great professors and advisors. Learning to connect is to begin a lifelong skill. Studies show that relationships you form in college often provide a launching pad for long-term careers. Whoever sat next to you in geology and studied for the exam with you in history could help you find a new job years later, when you really need it. The first step is just saying hello, smiling, and starting a conversation. That simple step can grow into a friendship, a business, or another kind of dream. All great students are expected to take that kind of initiative. If you choose not to take the initiative, you could graduate college with a degree, but with no network of friends and mentors to make that degree work for you. If that is all you get from all the time, effort, and expense of college, you have to ask whether the investment is worth it.

> ### People You Should Know Well on Campus
>
> - *Your academic advisor*
> - *Your resident assistant*
> - *Your professors and graduate assistants*
> - *Your career counselors*

> ### Places You Should Visit
>
> - *Library and study areas*
> - *Student union*
> - *Career center*
> - *Health center*
> - *Financial aid office*

Chapter 3
Making Your Papers and Projects Work for You

In the middle of difficulty is opportunity.

—*Albert Einstein*

The way you value yourself often determines your experience in college. You will truly transform yourself if you are willing to step up and master the opportunities ahead of you in your classes. You can identify and focus on interests that may open new worlds for you. In the process, you will grow in both intellect and courage.

RITES OF PASSAGE

In primitive societies, adolescent boys were initiated through physically demanding, arduous trials in order to take their roles as brave men in the tribe. Today, we have different rites of passage. Our modern rites are literacy-based, not physical. College is, in effect, our survival ritual by which we assume our place in the world as responsible adults. We prove ourselves by our ability to survive and thrive intellectually through our advanced ability to read, think, and write. Oral exams, essays, and papers are trials to demonstrate our ability to analyze, research, understand, and display our knowledge. But there is more to it than just surviving; there is also our need for discovery. We hope to be able to contribute fresh and useful ideas. We want to make a difference.

DEVELOPING A DOUBLE AGENDA

You may think of college as separate from the outside world, but it is quite a microcosm. Everything that you need or want from the real world is right here in college for you to experience and try. Don't settle for merely fulfilling requirements. If you use college to generate rich opportunities, you will find it far more interesting and valuable.

Be the experimenter. If you turn college into your own personal laboratory, you will find yourself and discover new ideas to pursue. You will be able to develop skills and awaken a passion for subjects that might well turn into a career. You can create strategies for realizing the work that can bring you happiness, value, and connection—ideas that will define your next world. It will be your most revolutionary act only if you are brave enough to turn your college life into your real rite of passage.

Taking tests and writing papers can be much more than just hoops to jump through. If you allow it, this very process will give you skills you can build on and count on later in life. You can make these mandatory tasks serve two important functions for you and double your rewards. You can perform the required task and then extend the assignment in order to explore your own interests and develop expertise. In other words, if you do more than the course requires—merely passing the test or writing the essay—and link the assignment to what you are interested in, you will create another level of experience.

> *Repeat endlessly to yourself, "It all depends on me."*
> —André Gide

Using Papers to Discover Your Interests

Whether they are long or short, papers offer you a direct way to develop your own double agenda. Besides meeting the requirements set by the professor for the course, you can use papers as a path to discover your own passions. Sometimes you already know your passions or have inklings about them, but often not. If you don't have a clue, use the course requirements as the way to find your own spark. If you allow yourself to be triggered by some project that engages your curiosity, a single *college course* can help guide your *life course*. It can ignite the search for your own treasure: finding your purpose and finding a path that will let you contribute through your act. These acts may just turn into your life's work.

Your professors' requirements are the first step in this treasure hunt. They will give you a topic or a list of topics to choose from and may tell you what they expect, perhaps with some guidance on how to conduct your search. Figuring out what *you* want from an assignment is much harder, especially at first, than just choosing the topic that seems easiest. "Quick and dirty" is one way to do these tasks, but the joke is on you if you take that route, because even "quick and dirty" takes time and effort. If you are bored or trying to rush, you are losing out.

Stop and really think about matching your own curiosity and interest to the list of topics given. If nothing beckons to you, ask if you can create your own topic, and argue for that if necessary. One obvious objective is a good grade, of course. Most everyone wants that. But, what else? Take the time to think about the outcome you could wish for by the end of the course. Look beyond the semester's course load and consider what you really hope for from your program. You are paying for the course; get your money's worth.

Here's an example. A group of MBA students was mired down in their team project, an analysis of supermarkets. I asked whether any of them was interested in supermarkets. They confessed that none of them was. How, then, did they choose the topic in the first place? It was simply last on the list; no other team had picked it. Unsurprisingly, they were bored and frustrated, but the clock was ticking. I asked each one of these students, who all worked full-time jobs, what they would like their next job to be. When one said he would like to work in pharmaceuticals, I had a plan. I pointed out that since all supermarkets have pharmacies or designated aisles for over-the-counter drugs, why not write about how markets select which drugs to sell, or how the grocery displays them, or how they take into account customers' preferences? Perhaps they could interview a series of salespeople, market managers, or customers, either individually or in a focus group. With these suggestions as a guide, the team grew more interested. They wrote a paper that not only got them As, but also added marketing skills to their résumés. Not a bad outcome for a team that selected the topic no one else wanted!

Writing is no fun. It's only fun to have written. —*Dorothy Parker*	**A Writing Tip** Writing a paper is deceptively hard work. First comes choosing the topic. Sounds simple, but it isn't. You are probably used to picking a topic from a list and filling in the blanks or piecing together other people's research.

These methods work well the first few times, but they don't get you closer to your core goals.

Instead, try this: imagine that the topic you choose will lead you to your dream job. Choose to investigate any part of the topic that will bring you closer to that world—researching the subject or interviewing practitioners. Pick something you care about, then write one paragraph to explain it, months ahead of the deadline. Outline it the second week; flesh out the outline with a page, even a chapter. Pull it together with an introduction and a conclusion. Now you have your first draft. While most students would turn that in, don't do that. Read your paper aloud to yourself and listen for what you forgot to write; find redundant explanations, unclear phrasing, and transitions you may have left out to guide the reader from one thought to another. You'll easily hear what is missing, what is repeated, what is not thoroughly explained.

Why can't the first draft work? Because writing requires mental discipline, exercising an interior brain muscle. It's as unrealistic to expect that you can do it well the first time as it is to think that you can run a marathon the first time you put on your sneakers, or to paint a masterpiece with your first brush stroke. The skill lies in the efforts to rewrite. You'll be writing all your life. And your ability to do it well makes a huge difference in almost any career you choose. Not only writers, but the most accomplished scientists, artists, managers, and entrepreneurs, all write about their ideas. Rise above the mediocre writing skill, and you'll be well ahead.

But don't cheat. Plagiarizing is stealing other people's work and passing if off as your own. It is your job to read others' work and turn their ideas into your own words. Cite your sources from the library's books or periodicals or online sources. Don't think you can fool your professors; they have not only read all the source material, they also know the level of your own writing ability.

Is the process of learning how to write fun? Not in the way you are used to thinking of "fun." All writers agree, and complain, that writing is really rewriting. Sometimes you get over the agony of thinking and get free of a state of confusion. Sometimes you can get into the flow so that the writing proceeds with very little effort. When that magic happens, you are in the flow of the great creative process, the nirvana that artists and imaginative people often experience.

The Zero-to-One Rule

Getting ready to start something is so much harder than continuing to do something. You have to get past all the fears of failing (and succeeding) to enter the work, which, ironically, is always easier. No matter where you are in your college career, you can use your curriculum to start developing your own specialization. Ideally, this will be something that compels you to further exploration—something that you may intend to build your career around. Make that topic the theme of your major and even the direction of your course work. You can delve into different facets of your theme in every course that requires you to submit a paper. This is the double vision at work: you are gaining expertise in an area that is compelling to you while also getting academic credit!

Your willingness to take that first step toward maturity and independence is the key to making opportunities that would otherwise not exist for you. You can begin this process by attending conferences to hear experts and become inspired to present your findings. Whether you are a grad or undergrad, working with a professor may allow you to have coauthorship, an auspicious beginning to a professional career.

For graduate students, the idea of building on a professor's work is especially valuable as you search for topics for your own theses and dissertations. But there is nothing stopping you undergraduates from engaging in research as well. In fact, this type of collaboration can be a great spur to any undergraduate who intends to continue to graduate school. Every professor to whom I've spoken agrees with this point, and each has been instrumental in guiding interested undergraduates by helping them plan and prepare for graduate programs. Cal Tech, for example, has a special summer program to let students do just that in science, and so do many private and state universities across the country. Most graduate programs are more likely to accept students who have already done some significant research or even published articles, because those students were the most likely to continue.

> Talent is what you possess. Genius is what possesses you.
> —Malcolm Cowley

GO FORWARD WITH PROJECTS

Every course has its requirements—usually papers and exams, but sometimes projects. Occasionally, you are able to substitute a special project for the more common exam or paper. If you can, do it, because projects offer unique possibilities for you to explore interests firsthand and develop connections to the outside world.

If, for example, you are enrolled in business or management school, you can also learn to design surveys to cover such subjects as the philosophy of work, emerging employment, trends, comparative studies in productivity, the impact of new technologies and resulting new products, or the training of new workers. By interviewing managers or employees at a company and then sharing your results, you reap several benefits. Besides learning from these experiences, your commitment will show how you work and think. You can also invite several of the most impressive people you meet to your class to relate their experiences and ideas. After you complete your project and discover your interest in this aspect of information gathering, you can follow up by contacting the marketing, advertising, or human resources departments of that company, which will certainly give you an edge for future employment.

A project for a Harvard MBA program was to develop a workable business plan. One student combined his personal knowledge of his family's discount pharmacy business with his keen interest in books and created a plan for the first discount bookstore chain. Not only did that project satisfy his program requirements, but it led to starting his own business, Crown Books, a company that revolutionized the discount bookselling industry in precomputer days.

The real voyage of discovery consists not in seeking new landscapes, but in having new eyes.
—Marcel Proust

Double Agendas That Launched Careers

I learned about making college help me find my calling only when I was enrolled in my doctoral program. I didn't have a clue about using the curriculum to develop myself and to forge a career based on my own interests when I was an undergraduate English major at Penn or a master's candidate in English. By chance, I met an inspired man, Sam Scheele, and joined his social engineering firm to manage a year-long conference helping people to identify an ideal project and commit themselves to make it manifest. I listened to what people wanted, helped them hone their ideas, found answers and expert advice to guide them, and celebrated their successes. By the end of this intense project, I realized that this work was my calling. To learn how people really succeed, I enrolled in the innovative doctoral Change Management Fellowship Program at UCLA. Only then, with such a passionate focus, could I make each course's assignments a means for me to explore the subject that had become my own mission: identifying other people's career skills. For example, in a history of ideas class, I had to persuade my professor to let me trace the fifty-year history of how-to literature—a particularly American genre of success in relationships and careers—and how it changed over time. For my concentrated classes, I began to chronicle the identification of skills for success through workshops, comparing the stories of accomplished and fulfilled people to those who made excuses for their failure to achieve as they had hoped. I studied how people choose their dreams and make them come true. I chose a brilliant group of professors for my dissertation committee, with Helen S. Astin as chair, and was encouraged to write *Careering: Critical Career Competencies from Everyday Lawyering.*

I interviewed forty-seven highly successful law-trained people in Southern California. I asked them detailed questions about their lives, from their current practices to childhood experiences. I mapped four areas I was interested in: childhood, early adolescence, college and law school, and their career lives. Astonishing answers kept repeating themselves; I could not help but see a clear pattern. Without exception, every single lawyer was highly active in college. Not only did they do well academically, but they were all significantly engaged in their undergraduate education. They became student body officers and presidents of their fraternities. They were active in clubs such as drama, music, and debate. They wrote for and edited their campus newspapers. They played on and/or managed athletic teams. They each named professors who had mentored them.

In law school, many of them wrote for the law review. I didn't understand the significance of writing for this journal until I asked questions about where they wrote their articles. Then each one revealed that they changed their habits. While at first they all had chosen to write in a quiet place, the library or their rooms, they came back to write in the law review office because that was where the action was. "Action" meant time talking to the law review sponsor, the most connected professor in the school. "Action" meant being mentored by this revered professor, a far different experience than just sitting in a class of 500, anonymously, with no relationship at all with the professor. And mentored these successful lawyers were—not just for that year, but over their lifetimes.

That effort of establishing a double agenda throughout my coursework—for my requirements and for myself—grew from my dissertation topic to my first book, *Skills for Success.* From the process of a book tour, I landed a syndicated newspaper column, a career column in *Working Woman* magazine, a talk radio show on KABC, career segments on NBC's *Today Show,* ABC's *Good Morning America,* and CNBC, and now *Success Minutes* on the radio. That dissertation led to my work in career coaching and to international public speaking. Every step, traceable to that one paper, has been valuable.

Through work and through my doctoral program, I rediscovered my own particular passionate pursuit, one that has continued throughout my life. I have found patterns of life skills that make people satisfied, happy, contributing, and successful—from lawyers, to managers, educators, engineers, and artists, as well as *students*. I must admit that I had no inkling about any of this when I started out as a college freshman. I never expected any of this to happen, but I went after it all anyway. If I can, you can too.

I recognized the transforming power of college and graduate school. Higher education offers you the chance to have quality time with professors and great thinkers whose brilliance can direct or redirect your lives. College is a time to forge such relationships. It is a time for experimenting with ideas and leadership in clubs, activities, and new programs. It is the truest training ground. College can be a catalyst for your life, if you pursue it that way and you are willing to be active and give up a more passive role of just following instructions. My hope is to plant the seeds of engagement that lead to greater risk-taking and connection-building. That is what I can offer you.

It is up to you to flex your own mental and heart muscles, even if you don't know what you want in college or when you "grow up." Most people are not sure about what path to follow, and that is not in itself a bad thing. But you do have to experiment to find your path and let go of assumptions of what you "should" do. Experimenting means sampling compelling courses and activities and matching them with your desires.

Suppose you are an art education major wondering if you wouldn't be better off working in a business organization rather than teaching. Here are some ideas to help you clarify your choices and recognize that you can use the same talents and skills in a variety of careers. You might look into designing training aids, computer graphics, or management training programs. Find out what these careers are like by using assigned papers from your major or other classes to do the following:

- Research the history and success rates of training aids or programs.
- Compare product differences and similarities within one field, such as education, with others, such as the banking, museum, or computer fields.
- Volunteer to work, paid or not, on an actual design project.
- Interview local artists, graphic artists, or Web designers to find out how they exhibit and sell their work.
- Take electives in related fields, such as design, computer graphics, or communication theory, or take courses in training or in the arts.

If you investigate the possibilities latent in various assignments, your course work and related activities will become personally challenging and engaging. They may launch you into a field that is a perfect fit for you. Pursuing this kind of double agenda permits you to develop aspects of your major or specialty before you graduate and helps you choose a program that's really right for you. There is wisdom in building onto your natural abilities rather than forcing yourself to fit what others think is the right course of action.

Not doing these things is wasting an opportunity. What's the value of that? You'll have to make up for it later.

Fred's Story: Double Major, Double Agenda

Class assignments can be springboards to finding interests that can lead you to an exciting career.

Fred has a double major in history and business. A good writer, he doesn't have any idea what he'll do after graduation. He could tap into the subjects that interest him and generate ideas that can be refined into a career later on. For example, he could offer to write a history of the growth of a particular business and learn business writing in the process. If the paper is really good, the company might publish it in its newsletter or help to get it published elsewhere. Because he has demonstrated his interest and work, Fred has a good chance of being hired for the public relations or communications department of that company or for a newspaper or business service.

The paper, which earns Fred academic credit anyway, could also be the vehicle to a new career in itself. It might catapult Fred into a career writing company histories or as a writer producing annual corporate reports. It might lead to other related fields. But Fred will never know unless he is willing to extend himself for the assignment. Take assigned papers seriously. Find a topic that is personally engaging and actively research it. It is part of what makes college so worthwhile.

THE ABD DILEMMA

Imagine this degree: ABD—All But Dissertation. You may never have heard of it, but this is the most depressing degree and a too common one. Many brilliant graduate students pass all the required courses in their master's or doctoral programs but never start or finish their thesis or dissertation. This is evidence that students haven't learned to self-assign. They may have received excellent grades for doing all the assigned work but don't have a clue about independent thinking. Don't let this happen to you! Learn how to write when you are an undergraduate. Ask your professors for help, just as you would a coach, so that you can trust yourself in selecting a topic that matters to you. Then you can ask for help in the development of that idea. It's hard work, but it will pay off.

If you don't connect yourself to college, you waste time, money, and effort. But doing so can be the first time for real personal direction-finding, an education of the mind and the heart. The lesson lies inside you: find something that beckons and compels you, and pursue it. If you can't identify such a thing immediately, start a search. Talk to your professors and counselors about finding a promising lead. Professors and counselors are there to act as signposts for you, pointing out paths to investigate according to your interests. You have to start with a topic at hand—one that can lead somewhere. Often, making yourself go through the process of pursuing a topic awakens buried interests or creates new ones. Strange as it may sound, many people don't pursue things they are interested in. But when you follow what you are drawn to, the payoff will be happiness and fulfillment in a career down the road. You don't want to end up like the regularly surveyed majority of people who report that they are unhappy with their work.

Writing usually involves not only creating the initial draft, but making repeated revisions. A gifted psychology student wrote a paper for her class and her professor told her to submit it to a journal. She did, but when it came back, the editor requested some changes. The student had never been asked to revise anything and didn't want to put in the effort. You can bet she regrets not doing it. She could have received a fellowship worth $12,000 per year instead of having to pay the full cost of tuition. Learning to revise papers is a critical skill you will use the rest of your life. Learn it now.

Every paper you write for a professor requires time and effort, so why not put in a little extra effort and make it count doubly? Write your paper for two goals: for your professor and the grade, of course, but also for possible publication in a professional magazine, journal, or newspaper. One liberal arts senior wrote a history of jazz and showed it to her father, a musician, who was so impressed with it that he submitted it to a West Coast jazz journal. They, in turn, published her paper in a seven-part series and offered her a job as well. Her friends said she was lucky that she had connections. Yes, she was. But she was more—she was plucky. Without doing more than was required, her job would not have happened.

Phil's Story: The Psych Graduate Student Who Wasn't Psyched

Tired of graduate school and eager to get to work, Phil, a psychology student, still had to face writing a dissertation. Instead of picking a subject that interested him or was related to the work he wanted to do, Phil chose a topic he thought would easily satisfy his professor. Then he undertook the usual laborious task of programming data—data that, in this case, he didn't care about but still spent many tedious hours analyzing.

The result was predictable. He wrote an indifferent first draft that was turned down by his professor. He put off the final draft because he was so bored. Now, Phil is a good candidate for that all-too-common degree, the ABD (All But Dissertation). This nondegree typically goes to "good students" who haven't learned the self-reliance that allows them to choose topics that will work for them. Our psychology grad student will need a lot of motivation to jump-start his stalled career. If he doesn't, he'll brand himself a failure and live with downsized expectations the rest of his life.

PAPERS THAT LAUNCHED PEOPLE

Whether you are in undergraduate or graduate school, you have to write a major paper. To build toward it, you can start with class assignments you already have, writing about aspects or segments of what your planned thesis might be. Once you've identified a topic that captures your interest, you've likely caught on to your real calling. Sometimes your research efforts can be transformed into a popular or commercial success. Examples abound: Deborah Tannen's *You Just Don't Understand*, Beverly Kaye's *Up Is Not the Only Way*, or my first book, *Skills for Success*.

A political science undergraduate in California studying the Middle East situation came up with an unusual solution for one aspect of its political strife. She sent her idea to the Op Ed (opinions and editorials) page of the *Christian Science Monitor*. The paper printed it. Even more rewarding, a professor at a fine eastern university read it and was so impressed with her fresh ideas that he offered her a fellowship to study with him in a special master's program. She accepted enthusiastically. By having the courage to write and then to "risk" submitting her paper in the first place (without any *real* risk), she set off a chain of events that could not have occurred if she had been content to sit back and settle for just a good grade.

The Teach for America program, which has put thousands of recent college graduates to work in underprivileged schools throughout the country, sprang from Wendy Kopp's senior thesis at Princeton. Kopp modeled her thesis program on the Peace Corps' two-year service. Teach for America has since won presidential approval to join AmeriCorps, former President Clinton's national service initiative. Wendy's goal transcended fulfilling an assignment; she wanted to solve a nationwide need for teachers while creating leaders. In the process, she created an impressive and meaningful career for herself.

Going Beyond the First Draft

In college, you write your papers once, turn in that draft, and wait for your grade. Like most students, you believe that is all there is to it. Yet all successful writers agree writing is rewriting. Because you are not usually required to rewrite your papers, you don't get the opportunity to learn how to refine your thoughts. If you are brave enough to want to learn more, let me offer an important (although often painful) strategy: discuss your paper with your professor. Go over the structure and details together. Learn how to rethink your ideas and rewrite them, *even though a second draft was not assigned, and even though you might not be given credit.* Do it anyway. In the process, you will learn how to develop and shape ideas. You will also become closer to your professor. Yes, it's hard work, but it's great work, and it will pay off in unbelievable ways! If you are interested in writing more creatively, take courses in writing or journalism to help you learn how to think more deeply and develop something that writers call their "voice."

Less obvious but just as important, rewriting will teach you how to put aside your immediate ego needs for something that will become far more valuable to you and stand you in better stead throughout your working life. One reason many companies don't want to hire new graduates is that they come to work with the same attitude that they had in school—a "once is enough" syndrome. In every aspect of life, from college to career, doing and redoing are what it takes to develop the discipline required to do a job well. Make yourself get as much experience as you can.

THE ADVANTAGE OF BEING A STUDENT: PEOPLE ARE OPEN TO YOU

You have a very real but invisible advantage as a student. Most successful people feel an obligation to assist you while you are in college. They want to help you, make time for you, share their work stories, and will answer your questions as soon as you identify yourself as a student earnestly studying something related to their business. When you identify yourself as a student on assignment, you are treated differently than a competitor or industrial spy. You have access to many kinds of information not usually revealed to other inquirers. Use this as an advantage to further your awareness about procedures, markets, inventions, and research.

The reality is that opportunities do not come labeled. They are disguised as obstacles or hard work and are only clearly identifiable in hindsight. Opportunities require a combination of risks and mental muscle. Start now.

CHOOSING ELECTIVES FOR SUCCESS

Just as there are behavioral skills to be developed, so are there interests and purposes to pursue. Typically, you do not know what your interests are all at once; rather, they are gradually uncovered. You confirm your interests through the choices you make and the actions you take to claim your mission in life. Keep this in mind when you're choosing electives. If you are an English major whose hobby is cooking, consider taking nutrition courses to increase the chances of being a food or cookbook editor or writer, or even a food stylist for commercials. If you are a science major, you may want to understand organizational theory as well as the theories of physics or biology. Take business courses as electives. If you are an urban planning major, know that much in your field depends on persuasive negotiation and presentations before groups. Take speech and debate courses to develop your presentation skills.

Learn to pay attention to developing your interests, whether they are small inklings or full-fledged passions. Allow yourself the pleasure of pursuing that which beckons you. Think of electives not as easy ways out, but as ideal ways to enhance your course of study with interests that make you happier and more well rounded; you will be more connected to your feelings. To ignore your own interests is to lose yourself while you pretend to be someone else. That someone will only disappoint you.

EXAMS, ANXIETY, AND SELF-PRESENTATION

Let's talk about exams, that college phenomenon that probably causes more anxiety than anything else. Tests appear as regularly as clockwork, yet somehow taking them doesn't get any easier. Except for those few who are ultra-confident, fear of being tested is profound. Students are afraid they will not look good or won't appear smart. They fear falling short of the expectations of an authority. This desperation can stop you from realizing what you do know and how well you can think. Despite the emotional strain, taking a test is still an ideal way to present what you have learned. From that point of view alone, they are valuable.

But there is another aspect of taking exams that is more subtle but equally important for establishing your double agenda. This second aspect is learning how to present yourself on paper as well as in person. Of course, I am not talking about objective tests such as multiple-choice. For those tests, there is only one piece of advice I can offer: find out as much about the test in advance as you can. Talk to someone who has previously taken a test given by the same instructor. Practice with test samples so that you are familiar with the format. Search for patterns in answering. This information is easily accessible for required standardized exams, such as the GRE, LSAT, or GMAT, from the test makers' regularly released sample test. Also, there is great help available in books, in electronic programs, from tutors on campus, and through test preparation courses.

Essays and subjective tests, however, are quite a different matter. You must demonstrate your critical thinking ability to your professors. The trick is not to answer like a student robot, spewing out meaningless lists of data, but instead to offer a conceptual framework that shows that you are knowledgeable and can take a larger view.

Presenting facts within a defined framework requires skill. Some students who regularly get As on their papers introduce their answers with a contemporary or classical theorist's quote or literary reference containing the essence of their response. By doing so, they demonstrate their ability to comprehend the material, to relate it to what has gone before, and to provide a graceful opening. It will be clear that they have taken the time before the test to do some research and include the views of theorists, thereby showing a grasp of both past and contemporary thinking. If the student has a preference for one school of thought over another, he or she will explain the reasons. In short, these students demonstrate in writing to their professors that they not only have a knowledge of their material, but also that they understand its significance.

Oral Exams: Worse Than a Root Canal?

For most people, speaking in public brings up the most terrible of fears. In fact, for some, fear of public speaking ranks ahead of being shot, mugged, or swindled! It's hard to believe that we are more afraid of what others think of us than what others will do to us. Simply being visible seems to expose us to danger. This is strange because there is no objective danger to speaking to a group; nevertheless, the feeling is there. However, there are ways to prepare ourselves so that we can appear to be as smart as we are.

Get practice. Take classes on debating and public speaking to think better and faster on your feet as well as to be seen as a leader. Make yourself take such courses, even though they seem formidable. Going through the typical trauma of speaking in front of a class is actually quite therapeutic; everyone is in the same boat and encourages each other. Public speaking provides invaluable training now and later on in your career. Every president, CEO, politician, and lawyer has this skill. Successful people become spokespersons for their companies, their industries, and frequently in their communities. They are rewarded for presenting themselves with strength and grace, whereas others who are equally talented, but shy, don't. Learning confidence in public early in college is one of the traits that successful people share. Of course, it helps enormously if you are sure that you really know your topic and can answer questions that may come up. It's a good exercise to visualize yourself in front of a large audience, telling them something they need to know, feeling very confident. Remember, we're dealing in your *feelings* as a speaker as well as the *facts* you will be presenting.

Rehearsing for Your Oral Exam

There are several tactics that you can use to improve your skills when you must endure an oral exam. This sort of exam is closely related to a job interview. First, rehearse by yourself in advance. Think of all the possible questions that your professor(s) might pose. Then prepare *comprehensive* answers. You cannot answer in monosyllabic yes's or no's anymore than you can get away with "I don't know." Even if you don't know an answer, begin your response by admitting that, elaborate on how you would go about finding out, and discuss where it fits into what you do know. Grunts, shrugs, and meandering don't cut it. Be fully alive and high in energy during the exam.

The rule: Tests have two aspects: demonstrating your mastery of the subject and choosing an appropriate style in which to provide the answers.

You can practice your oral answers, just as you would written answers. Format an oral answer just as you would an essay: create a beginning, middle, and end. You certainly should refer to the work of others, including that of the professor(s) you are addressing. It shows that you have conscientiously attended class and have taken the assignments seriously.

If you are a graduate student preparing for your orals, then you must also take responsibility for the exam session. What you are being judged on is not only whether you can remember all the small details, but also whether you can present your facts in a meaningful framework and in a cogent order. Let me repeat an incident, which was often misunderstood, that I included in *Skills for Success*. It's quite appropriate here.

A director of training of a major psychoanalytic institute told me about two young men who had just taken their oral examinations in order to be admitted to the institute. That means that about ten to twelve years after college, medical school, an internship, residency, their own psychoanalysis, and several years of special training in the institute, these two men were again tested to see if they were qualified to be admitted to the institute.

You might assume, as I did, that they would both pass since they had the same years of training. But only one of the two did. How was it possible for the other to fail after so much extraordinary education and practice? I asked the director to tell me the questions he asked of the two men as well as both the passing and failing responses. What I found out reveals the core of the all-important nature of self-presentation.

There was only one question: a tip-off in itself. It was asked of both men independently: "What would you expect a one-year-old baby to do if its mother, upon bringing it to your office, had to leave the room for a few minutes?" I asked for the *failing* response first; here it is: "I'd expect the baby to cry after being separated from the mother." I was surprised but didn't say anything except to ask for the *passing* answer: "I'd expect the baby to cry after being separated from the mother. Separation anxiety is maybe the most complex issue of all our lives, especially obvious in infancy. There are, however, conflicting interpretations. According to these...." Aha. Now I really got it!

Let's look at what happened. At first glance, it appears that the psychiatrists' answers are identical. The fact is there; both agree that the baby cries. But any important interview or exam doesn't measure only your ability to state a fact. *Facts* themselves are often less important than the *interpretation* of them, especially in the art of psychiatry. The failing psychiatrist gave an answer and then waited for a reaction. The passing one presented the same answer but then revealed what it meant through a series of interpretations. He provided a way to let the examiner know that he was prepared and had studied and read others' work extensively. Most importantly, he spoke as a colleague and as a likely credit to the institute. He knew intuitively that the test was a vehicle for such self-presentation.

The examiners, like most professors and employers, really want to ask "Are you enough like us to warrant our letting you join our institute?" The first psychiatrist was not; he proved himself still a student, waiting for the next question—which, alas, never came. But the second

> *Success is to be measured not so much by the position that one has reached in life as by the obstacles which he has overcome.*
> *—Booker T. Washington*

candidate showed himself to be their equal. In addition to knowing the fact, he also knew how to substantiate his answer with examples from psychiatric theory and practice. The director intuitively realized the difference between the two answers and consequently between the applicants; he chose the colleague to join him, not the student. But he could not tell me why; he could not tell the failing candidate why either.

All subjective tests, whether written or oral, are vehicles for self-presentation. The questions are there to provoke a dialogue, which is a vehicle giving you an opportunity to reveal who you are and what you know. These tests are all graded by someone looking for a person just like him or her to join the club, whether a class, college, or company.

You want not only to be a successful student, but also a successful protégé and thereafter a successful professional. Clearly you cannot wait until the last minute to learn the appropriate behaviors. These behaviors are social skills, and skills have to be developed, just as in sports. If you want to be an expert skier, would you put on a pair of skis and ski down the Jackson Hole vertical slope for the first time? Of course not. Yet that is exactly what we demand of ourselves when we come unprepared in high-pressure tests, written or oral. You need practice and coaching. Both are free and available to you. It is up to you to get them.

CONCLUSION: STRATEGIES FOR CREATING A DOUBLE AGENDA

Here are some tips for using academic assignments strategically, instead of just being passive, choosing the path of least resistance, and squandering your time:

1. If it is required, do it. But do it with heart.
2. If the assignment is harder than ones you are used to, talk to your professor about ways to attack the problem. Even though it feels awkward to ask for help, you are more likely to pull through, a far better alternative to failing. Something else you might not have

realized actually comes into play: your professor is likely to become more invested in your efforts to succeed and will offer more help and understanding.

3. If you can't complete the assignment or take the test because of some real emergency, make yourself go to your professors. Don't just fail to show up or let deadlines go by. If you leave a message but your professor does not call back, call her or him again and again; go to his or her office again and again until you make contact and complete your work. Don't ignore this seemingly unpleasant task of explanation and negotiation with your professor, or it will cost a lot more than you think.

4. A worst-case scenario? Failing a test or an assignment. Ask how you can make it up, take it over, or complete another one. Don't ignore it or give up because you are embarrassed. Turning failure around may be one of those events that you realize, only later (perhaps much later), helped you to grow.

5. Sometimes your past record is no reflector of your present ability. You might have goofed off in high school or, more likely, in your freshman year, but now you can change yourself and become a great student. Each semester you can make a fresh start. Do it now and do it excellently.

6. Ambition is a great stressor; use its adrenaline!

Chapter 4
Developing Your Best Self: Using Campus Clubs

*Action may not always bring happiness; but there is no happiness with-
out action.*

—Benjamin Disraeli

START WITH YOURSELF

The very definition of personality is debated. There are so many questions: Is it inherited or learned from people around us? How do you
develop a particular style? Can you modify your own personality, or does
it just emerge? Is your personality shaped by your family and friends, by
TV and movies, or are you some combination of all these factors? You
might agree that no matter how people develop our personality, they can
always modify aspects of it. Indeed, perople are more willing to change
their haircuts than modify anything about how they act. Most people,
therefore, act as if personality were given, fixed, not to be changed or
even challenged. The most successful people tell me over and over that
their success is due to their ability to adapt. Darwin theorizes that our
species survives because of this adaptive ability.

You can learn to modify your personality depending on the situation.
If you doubt that people change their behavior, then just think about
how you talk in one voice to your friends but in another to your parents,
one voice to your professors and another to your friends. You may sound

different and more persuasive when you are selling a car than when you are buying one. Our slipping into different characters or voices to fit the situation does not mean you do not have a real character. Far from it. Learning how to shift to be situation-specific indicates that you are healthy, savvy, and naturally adaptive. People choose what roles to enact, taking appropriate cues from the matter at hand. At first, you might think that this sounds manipulative. But it is much wiser to take charge of a situation than to be locked into only one way of acting. Simply carrying out your usual reactions like a robot removes the joy of spontaneous or reasoned reaction, not only for you, but also for the people around you.

Now that you are in college, you have already developed an initial sense of style in many ways. Take fashion, for example. You know what is appropriate according to the event and you choose appropriately whether you're going to a soccer match or an interview, whether it is summer or winter. You are not aware yet that you have already changed your style and that you will keep changing according to your status and opportunities that come your way. What you will wear for a first job will definitely be different from what you wear a few years later, when you are in a higher-level position. Fashion is one statement about yourself. Dressing well certainly won't get you into graduate school or guarantee that you'll get (or stay) hired for the job you want. However, you won't even be considered if you deviate much from the style norm. What counts more is something usually invisible to yourself but not to others: your behavior. By "behavior," I mean the presentation of yourself or how you show who you are in different situations.

But who or what is this self? Is it your account of who you are, what you have learned, or what you will contribute? And how do you develop a repertoire of personal behaviors? For the most part, we develop only one way of interacting—a "uniform of behaviors"—and, as a result, we are stuck acting that way for a lifetime. If you are obliging and unthreatening, you are considered sweet and supportive. Or, you can get stuck playing the aggressive, bad boy or girl. How, then, do you develop a more appropriate repertoire of personal behaviors?

Jim's Story: Engineering a Change

Here is an example of how a student's direction can shift if he is paying attention to where his interests lie. Jim was a top engineering student who wanted to be an engineer since childhood. His father shared and encouraged his son's dream of a career in engineering as a means of escape from a limited, rural background. Had he kept his early dream intact, blinded to any other possibility, he would be an engineer today. That is certainly not a bad choice, but good choices have more to do with combining abilities with personal interest.

Jim found that he was interested in student politics. Gradually, he got involved in student government and became a campus leader. His position required him to resolve and mediate conflicts between student officers, deal with a few unpopular issues, inform his sponsors and professors of the student body government decisions, and invite provocative guests to campus meetings. From the seemingly simple act of becoming a student body officer, Jim had discovered new potential in himself. He became a confident leader with a pronounced talent for management. He tried out a new role and succeeded in it.

There are usually some trade-offs in life. Jim did sacrifice straight-A grades and was afraid that he would lose his chance for the one engineering position that he really wanted. But, in fact, that company hired him because they were more impressed with his political experience than his GPA. They immediately placed him in a management program in one of the nation's most prominent organizations. Looking back, he realized that having been a student body president changed his entire life.

Developing a Repertoire of Behaviors and Roles

Cocurricular activities provide a safe place for you to begin to expand your behavior and practice participating and flexing your style. Through these activities, you learn how to behave in groups as a team player and as a star. If you increase your involvement, you will learn how to form and articulate an opinion, when to be persuasive and when not to be, when to take the lead and when to be supportive, how to handle conflict within a group and when to ignore it. Developing these skills is critical as the basis of your adult personal style. They are meta skills, life skills, skills you can start developing in college that will keep developing over your lifetime.

The Hidden Curriculum of Clubs and Activities

Clubs and activities, once called extracurricular, now are called cocurricular activities. The word "extra" suggested that these were not part of the real or academic curriculum and were, therefore, less than valuable. In reality, however, clubs and activities offer a hidden second curriculum that complements and expands on what you learn in the classroom. Clubs and activities teach you how to work on a project with people— something that can't be learned while listening to a lecture or researching in a lab. Because no one works in complete isolation in the real world, developing communication skills can be as important as the ability to do the job. Recruiters tell me repeatedly that these interpersonal skills are actually more important to them, because your engagement and leadership in cocurricular activities reveals how well you will perform in their organization.

It is worth the time to discover the cocurricular world that exists on your campus. You will find hundreds of clubs or events in which you can get involved. For example, think about the campus radio station and baseball team as possible activities. They offer programs that must be planned, budgets to sort out, advertising and publicity to create, and people to manage—in addition to the core roles of a DJ or catcher. You will learn as many relevant lessons for your future from being involved in any of these aspects as you will from the core roles. Gaining experience comes only from the actual doing. There is no shortcut for it. College is a safe place to start to practice these skills. Because getting fired from a club or activity is unlikely, you are free to experiment more than you would in a real job. And experimentation, a form of risk-taking, will be valued much more in your later work.

Here are leadership skills that you can learn from the "hidden curriculum" of clubs and activities:

- Motivating and influencing a group to do more
- Negotiating skills to create win-win consensus and compromise— growing beyond always needing to be *right* at the expense of proving others *wrong*
- Learning and practicing the critical arts of collaboration and teamwork
- Sampling new career choices in a natural way

I led a recent focus group of employers, and every single one stressed the importance of the interviewee's participation in cocurricular experience. They identify and choose those students who have proven records of taking responsibility, being motivated, and displaying willingness to go beyond merely what is expected. A leading biotech company's slide presentation of qualities the company is searching for in recruiting thousands of excellent students listed team-building and communication skills at the top of the slide, before grades.

My interviews with successful people have repeatedly shown that almost no one becomes successful overnight. No matter whether they were businesspeople, artists, or scientists, their ability to make appropriate decisions—often forging critical turning points in their lives—was always based on earlier, preparatory steps they had taken. For many, actions they had taken in high school and college led to building their courage to take risks and to persevere through difficult times. Successful people whom I have observed have built their expertise through the years and continue to cultivate their skills and knowledge. They are always preparing for the next step, consciously or not, even if they do not know what that next step will be. Many of the highest achievers I interviewed credited their cocurricular activities for first developing their success strategies.

What is in a list of activities? While it is true that some students will join clubs only to add them to their résumés, the majority of achievers whom I interviewed always did much more than merely join. They all made something happen, no matter what situation they were in. And making things happen—actively partaking in the organizations—is a great skill in itself. It is the foundation of building personal courage and mastery.

At a dinner meeting for Martin Edelson's *Boardroom Reports*, I was seated next to Jane Brody, the great science columnist for *The New York Times*. I asked her about her college involvement and heard an astonishing story. From earliest childhood, she had wanted to follow in her father's footsteps and study science at Cornell. At eighteen, she had achieved her goal. But in her freshman year, she fell into a deep depression. A counselor suggested that joining a club would help. She agreed but would not leave her safety base, the science building. The only activity that was held inside was the science newsletter. Keeping her word, she joined. To her astonishment, she found her calling then and there: not doing science, but writing about it.

I had the pleasure of interviewing Eli Callaway, the marketing genius who led Burlington Industries to create the first synthetics, then developed the wine industry in Southern California, and finally invented the legendary golf club, Big Bertha. I asked him about his college activities at Emery. He said his father promised him a car if he would learn how to sell ads for the campus newspaper. He did just that. And, in the process, he got much more than a new car.

What You Will Work On

Learning how to create opportunities is a major life skill, and one that can be developed. A cautionary word: the extraordinary effort that real engagement requires is worth it, even if you have to defend your involvement to your friends or family for taking time away from your studies. The saying "If you want something done, ask a busy person" is completely true. You will become better at managing your time and become more efficient at studying. Cocurricular activities and clubs have proven to be the touchstones upon which many successful people have based their continuing experiences. Achievers specifically credit their college extracurricular activities for developing these various skills that stand them in great stead throughout their lives:

- Building personal courage
- Dealing cooperatively with peers and others
- Developing organizational savvy, the sense of how to engage well in "office politics"
- Establishing a first sense of real professionalism

These key factors are not typically taught in college, not even in MBA programs or law school, although they certainly belong there. Academic learning is slowly evolving to integrate a second curriculum that includes skills critical to real life. You will find evidence that it is happening on your campus with programs such as "service learning," which allows students to perform service work in the community as part of their academic coursework and first year experience, targeting needs of entering students.

Dramatic Results for Drama Club Members

Most of the successful lawyers I interviewed attribute their skills of persuasion to their early, active participation in a drama club. They said that acting helped them break out of their shells and be more aware of their audience or listeners. That lawyers are interested in acting should not be surprising; after all, the courtroom itself creates dramatic situations. It's also interesting to note that the personality type of courtroom lawyers and actors shows up as the very same in John Holland's vocational code, a revealing instrument to discover your aptitudes, which you can find in your career center.

Clearly, drama and improv clubs are good training not only for future lawyers and actors, but also for the rest of us. Drama club offers the same advantages for anyone who needs practice in overcoming performance anxiety and learning how to build a persuasive case—for getting into a closed seminar, winning a grant in science, having a building plan approved, convincing a supervisor that your project deserves priority, or persuading a potential client that your art is valuable. Acting skills are akin to selling skills. Acting also gives you the chance to memorize the lines of some of the greatest works of world literature, which are not always included in regular courses. In another interesting way, drama clubs offer an invaluable first step in career advancement: learning to overcome the fear of facing an audience.

Getting up to speak in public is one fearful act. You either shy away from it altogether or do it with your hands and knees shaking. Why are people so afraid of presenting their ideas to others? Being judged to be dumber than they look is the awful pain that stops them. You have to practice being before public groups and overcome your initial paralysis. Otherwise, you remain a victim, encased in your own private terror. The only way out is learning to stand up, speak up, and become visible and audible.

Participating versus Just Showing Up

What you get out of an activity depends on what you put into it. John joined the Future Teachers of America (FTA) club, even though he was not excited about becoming a member of what he regarded as a limited profession. Not only did he join with half a heart, he joined with only half a mind. Mentally absent during the meetings he attended, he went through the motions of being a member. He paid his dues and attended the meetings, but he sat in them like the proverbial bump on a log, volunteering nothing, chairing nothing, contributing nothing, asking nothing. After graduation, he was unable to find a teaching job that suited him. It was not that the field of education was a bad choice. It is that John did not take advantage of his chances.

Carol, the president of that same club, had an entirely different result. She applied for teaching positions in the public school system and at a community college system. Because she had already established a reputation prior to graduation, she was accepted by both school systems. How did she do this and not John when they both had the same GPA? The difference lies in how Carol got involved in the FTA. During her last few years, she invited guests, both teachers and department chairs, to speak to the club, and she stayed in contact with these people. She researched alternative curricula for colleges and wrote papers about them. She familiarized herself with the jobs of president, counselor, and instructor at liberal arts colleges and community colleges. She created opportunities for club members through a variety of internships. She sponsored a series of dinner meetings with faculty so that active students could learn more about the inside world of higher education. Finally, she asked the influential people she had come to know to write letters of rec-ommendation for her; they responded positively. Other students who didn't know her well attributed her first-time college teaching position to luck.

Compare these two antithetical experiences. John came to the club expecting to be "done to"—informed, educated, placed, and launched— while Carol came to create something and help build a successful group. The FTA, like any other organization, offers every member the same opportunities. One took advantage and benefited; the other did not.

If you want something to happen, you have to make it happen. Life is, indeed, what you make it. The philosopher Kierkegaard wrote that the irony of life is that we understand it only by looking backward, in reverse, but we are forced to live it out in forward gear. What we can do, how-ever, is to benefit from others' experiences through their perfect 20/20 hindsight to make us smarter.

Set up your own experiments. Include on your list: clubs and activi-ties, internships, part-time jobs, courses, and seminars. Seize as many chances as possible to shape and reshape yourself according to what you want most. Your success hinges on your willingness to try, even at the rel-atively minor risk of making a fool of yourself, in order to create your own possibilities.

While you can just sign up for a major, you actively choose your activities, which are typically based on your own interests. This may be the first time you come close to your own heart's desire; pay attention to your inner tuning fork of interest. Still, you have to work for it: you have to come to the club to try out, audition, push yourself to become more involved, perform in front of others, be criticized by your sponsor, take the heat from losing or the adulation from winning. You have to over-come your own inertia and conquer your passivity in the process.

A group of unemployed PhDs, graduates of a major institution, formed a support group, for no matter how hard they tried, they were unable to find what they yearned for and prepared so many years for—full-time teaching positions. They decided to make their plight public. They appeared on talk shows and were sympathetically interviewed in the local newspapers. They held monthly meetings and invited guest speakers to help them.

I was one such speaker and began by saying that, since we can't always get what we want, at least not at the beginning, we need to think of alternatives to keep us alive. I noticed that my presentation was being recorded. When I asked why, they said it was for publication in their initial newsletter. It seemed odd to me that they were moving from being a support group, to helping each other find work, to becoming an association with its own ambition. They wanted their association to expand in size and scope and to produce a comprehensive monthly newsletter. They were acting as if their group should grow and continue. Yet this was a group whose purpose should have been to dissolve once the members could find jobs! Perhaps a more productive course would have been getting into the career development business. If so, then they could have invited each member who did find work to come back with a list of what he or she actually did. They might have sought help in starting up a short internship program to fuse academic theory with business practice. They could have made some more helpful alliances, linking chemistry PhDs with oil companies, graphic arts grads to advertising agencies, and historians with libraries, magazines, or newspapers.

Why didn't they do this? As ivory tower academicians, they regarded the business of business with disdain. They were falling into the "good student" trap. Yet because universities were not hiring full-time professors, they desperately needed to reexamine their beliefs to become employed. Had they only used their university time more creatively and productively, allowing time for varied activities, they might well have had a broader view of alternatives. Had they participated in cocurricular activities, their connections and experiences might have provided the employment opportunities they sought.

DIRECTION FINDERS:
WHAT AM I GOING TO DO WITH MY LIFE?

Don't worry that you'll have only one chance to make a career choice that will hold for the rest of your life. The odds are that you can and will have several careers in your life. While change is predicted, you still may not know where to start first. Break the confusion and start by taking a risk and joining a club that interests you. By doing that, you will increase your knowledge of that subject, which, in turn, will help direct you in your career choice.

Simply start by finding what appeals to you now. After a month or two, then you can decide to what extent you want to be involved. You will find that participating in athletics and music is quite different from the production of a radio show or newspaper or running for a student political office. You will find that your participation will not be limited by your athletic ability or performing talents; rather, it will be enhanced by the actions you are willing to take. You have to develop team skills to be part of a group that can create harmony together, whether it is a jazz band, football team, or debating club. All of these activities offer the possibility of many different kinds of interpersonal experiences in addition to the theme.

An all-American basketball star told me that his greatest learning experience came, surprisingly, during the time when he was benched. Despondent during that difficult year, he nevertheless learned to cheer on his team members. Only after being there for them could he understand that a large part of his value and purpose came in supporting his team members, not just playing well himself. Any athletic team will comprise many roles: best performers, most valuable, most supportive, most popular. Each of these positions, in addition to that of the coach, the manager, and even the publicist, performs a vital role in the team's existence and success.

Understanding our talents and how we fit in is vital to our own development. But how do we learn these things? If you are a member of the band but not the leader, you still have many chances to contribute. You may be the one who finds unusual music, or the one who gets the campus newspaper to review the group, or the one who contacts professional musicians off campus to listen to and advise the group. Or you might be the one who cooks chili for the band and generates enthusiasm, helping to create real esprit de corps.

A campus newspaper or radio show offers a variety of jobs. If you are creative, you can be the writer, the performer, or both. If you are technical, you can be responsible for the sound and delivery. If you are interested in public relations and advertising, you can sell the production to the potential audience. If you are interested in management, you can make connections with professors, administrators, and the entire outside community. These activities can become virtual minibusinesses, as can fund-raising events, homecomings, and alumni weeks. And best of all, they lead directly to your dream career.

A group of students interested in studying business might start an investment club or a small enterprise, creating a perfect reason to seek out professors as advisors. In this way, the group can learn both how to relate and how to perform. At this very moment, all over the United States, students are playing the stock market, catering parties, publishing neighborhood guides, and moving other students in and out of apartments, as well as feeding them. Remember, college is its own laboratory. Within it exists a huge variety of opportunities for experiments of all kinds, from academic to entrepreneurial. And many professors, counselors, and administrators are willing to act as coaches.

These activities offer real chances to find out what you like and what you don't like, what you need to learn in addition to what you already know. If you discover you care more about creating and selling the concept by yourself than you do working with a team, you might lean toward entrepreneurship rather than a large corporate business environment. You might find that you prefer focused research. But only by experimenting with different roles and settings can you find clues toward answering that most perplexing of questions: "What am I going to do when I finish college?"

Using Preprofessional Associations

Many professional associations offer student memberships as well as sponsor professional clubs for students majoring in the field. There are associations for nearly every discipline—engineering, nursing, dentistry, teaching, chemistry, filmmaking. Getting to know professionals in the field provides a valuable source of contacts. Participating in regional and national conventions gives you a chance to see who's who in the profession and to keep current with technical developments and trends in the field.

A group of engineering students, holding a preprofessional seminar just before their national convention, invited me to conduct a workshop for the students. One of the engineering students caught my interest because of the quality of her questions and ideas. During the days of the national convention itself, I invited her to accompany me to some of its meetings and dinners. Her own charisma became evident to some of the practicing engineers. One of them gave her a lead that landed her a job in a chemical division of an excellent company. Since then, she has kept me informed of her subsequent career moves and successes, and I have enjoyed her letters and calls. Professionals and student sponsors all share this same sense of joy from watching a student take risks and grow. These actions, in turn, embolden all of us to take more chances in our own lives as well as encourage our friends, colleagues, and families to do the same.

Lessons for Leadership

Student government represents another major area for volunteer activity. Successful people who have entered a race for student office, regardless of whether or not they win, agree that the experience was much more worthwhile than they expected. First, they learned to risk their own egos. It takes courage to lay your ideas on the line and set yourself up for criticism as well as possible defeat, which is exactly what you do when you run for office. Second, they learned how to create a team of their supporters. It takes more courage to ask people not only for their vote, but also to campaign for you. Third, they learned how to be there when the votes are counted. If you don't win, you have to learn to be a gracious loser, congratulating your opponent and offering him or her your support. If you do win, then you must begin to act on your campaign promises. Winning is an honor, but it is hardly an end in itself; it is another beginning, a real chance to push forward and make things happen.

Coming through is a skill in itself to be practiced, tested, and realized. But it isn't enough. Leadership includes public speaking, which requires you to learn the skill of thinking on your feet. It also requires developing expertise in motivating others and directing functions or events and experience in striking compromises between opposing factions. Only with hands-on practice and experience can you understand the difficult process of leadership.

In assuming leadership roles in most student organizations, you have the privilege of working under the direction of a sponsor, who is usually someone savvy and connected. You can expect to have access to professors, administrators, alumni, other club presidents, and the outside world, with a much broader scope and greater ease than others might have.

Involvement in student government can, for example, lead to the larger political world. It might start with volunteer work on a politician's campaign and them move up to clerkships, internships, and even graduate school. It is no accident that many top executives, professionals, and community and national leaders, including presidents, were political leaders as college and graduate students. Ability to lead is one hallmark of an achiever. The skill that it takes can be developed and made a part of your repertoire.

Leadership is integrated into the social fabric of our society. So far we've talked about getting the top roles, but running for office yourself or chairing a committee is not the only way to develop political smarts. Learning how to support a designated leader is also critical.

Steve's Story: A Capitol Decision

Here's a good illustration of how involvement in student activities can help you find a direction.

Steve had been a student body president from junior to senior high school and from junior college to Cal State University at Northridge. After spending one year at Cal State without political involvement, he decided to live on campus and run for office, even though it added another year to his program. The mayor, hearing one of Steve's speeches, was so impressed that he invited him to intern with his staff. Proving himself in that internship, Steve won a senate fellowship, served on the senate staff in Sacramento, and learned how a bill makes it through and how lobbyists influence that process. These experiences made their mark. Steve discovered that his calling was public service.

If your own goal is to be a leader, you'll learn how to perform that role more effectively by assisting a leader first. If your goal is to be a good team player with far more chances, you'll get free practice sessions. You'll find out that a supportive role is not a passive one. Nobody makes it alone. Being supportive requires committed attention to the goals and behavior of the leader, to be sure, but also to the group and to the rest of the campus.

THE MAKING OF WOMEN LEADERS

A group of successful alumnae, graduates from Harvard, got together to discuss how they could support Harvard. Ironically, these women hadn't really gone to Harvard, because in the 1950s, Harvard matriculated only men. These women, therefore, went to Radcliffe, its sister college. Like many women, they found that Radcliffe, like other women's colleges, proved to be a safe haven to practice leadership skills and develop strong leaders.

They decided to pressure the current president of Harvard to hire more than the usual token number of tenured women professors, a sad statistic for most of the Ivies, in return for financial support. They tried but didn't get anywhere. Angered at their lack of progress, the group decided to put their money in a trust fund, stipulating that it could not be spent until more women were hired and promoted. They also swore that they would prevent their grandchildren from attending until equity was established. They had made their stand.

Equality for women from college and beyond is slowly happening, but it takes several generations to realize progress. In reality, women are still too often viewed in supporting roles as opposed to leadership roles. Old habits of thought and culture die hard. Change is resisted even by those of us who want it most. But we can prepare ourselves. We need to. The Department of Labor predicts that women and minorities will be filling two-thirds of all newly created jobs in the early part of the twenty-first century.

Boss Man? Boss Woman?

As a management consultant to large organizations, part of my work has been to train employees to be more productive and proactive. I have designed problem-solving exercises to develop initiative and leadership skills. In one of these exercises, I divided the participants into small groups without naming group leaders. Then I gave them an assignment of working in their groups to find the best solution to a hypothetical management problem. The assignment itself acts as the means to uncover the process. When the groups finished the assignment, I moved on to the critical point of the exercise. I asked the person who had emerged as the leader of each group to stand up.

Without exception, here's what happens: When the group is all-male, one man who played the leader role will immediately stand up. When I ask why he believes that he was the leader, he answers with the following list of roles: he initiated the discussion, took notes, shaped the format, kept the discussion focused, facilitated group participation, summarized the decisions, and accomplished the task within a given time. The same thing happens when a male is the leader in a mixed gender group. He stands up immediately, no false modesty about it, and recites the same litany of leadership roles.

But when the leader of a mixed group is female, typically she is reluctant to stand up in the first place and needs the active encouragement of her group to claim her leadership role. She doesn't seem to want to acknowledge her own power without her group's permission. When she does accede that she acted as the leader, she recites the very same activities as her male counterparts. It turns out that leadership is leadership, no matter the gender of the leader. Its traits are known and recognized. The only difference between genders is reluctance to claim the title.

But what about all-female groups? Invariably, one of the strongest women claims that the entire group participated equally without a leader. Consistently, this is what women say every time. But when I ask who has taken the responsibility for facilitating, guiding, redirecting, and focusing the group, one woman—usually the one who originally declared that there was no one leader—will finally stand.

Such an exercise offers insight into a remarkable process with definite patterns. There are few differences in the way men and women describe their leadership qualities. It isn't that women are less qualified to be leaders than men, because as leaders they perform the very same acts. The major difference lies not just in male reluctance to accept women as leaders, but also in women having a harder time, socially and psychologically, accepting themselves as leaders.

If you are a woman student, you will need to learn something besides your academic subjects: confidence in yourself. You need experience to gain confidence to achieve the following:

- Try difficult subjects and insist on belonging in those classes.
- Speak up in class rather than just waiting for a safer one-on-one discussion after class.
- Debate with an appropriate and authoritative voice.
- Resist being interrupted or engaging in self-censorship.
- Write a paper without feeling cut off from your own thoughts.
- Build respect and encouragement from your professors.
- Refuse to depend only on your physical attractiveness to carry you through.
- Report sexual harassment immediately if it happens, without fear.
- Don't feel the need to prove yourself over and over.

Let's look at what "proving" yourself means. At the core of most sexual harassment is expectation. Our society expects young men to do well in college and then in their careers. And they usually do. In fact, they have to really mess up to get expelled or fired. On the other hand, we don't expect the same of women; in fact, our society simply doesn't have the same expectations for women to do well. Women have been excluded from the kind of automatic belonging that men are heirs to. Therefore, to become accepted and valued as more than just competent, women have to keep proving that they can do the job, over and over, each time.

Yes, it's true that women have come a long way. The glass ceiling keeping women out of top management has been cracked a little more over the past several decades, a blink of history's eye, but there's much further to go. Numbers from the Department of Labor provide the surest measure of women's progress; men are still at least $20,000 ahead in professional salaries.

Is this difference fair to everyone, whether women or other "minorities?" Of course not. Its toll is the shattering of self-image. The issue of confidence sometimes gets lost in a chicken-and-egg issue of which came first, women's lack of confidence or their lack of equal opportunity? Ultimately, the cause doesn't matter. People change their destiny by changing themselves from the inside out. To overcome their own reluctance, women have to look for specific opportunities to practice assertive living. Some call it leadership, others call it personal mastery. But it won't change only by law or with time. Women must keep making themselves more able, and they can begin that process by signing up for preprofessional associations.

If we do not pitch our discussions of right livelihood to enlightenment, we have failed to give work its true dimension, and we will settle for far too little—perhaps for no more than a living wage.
—Theodore Roszak

LEARNING ESSENTIAL LEADERSHIP SKILLS NOT TAUGHT IN CLASS

To develop more confidence in learning new skill sets, join cocurricular activities and clubs. Sign up for one committee, then step up your involvement by running for office (preferably sooner than your caution may dictate). You'll learn initiative and develop people skills, such as motivating others, resolving conflicts, and solving problems. You'll build leadership and team skills that involve knowing how to be a team player as well as a star. You'll make and take your rightful place.

An engineering and math major, dulled by the imbalance of studying quantitative subjects only, decided to join a club devoted to philosophical discourse. To his surprise, he found his home on campus among other students whose majors, like his, did not include such intellectual intimacy. Twenty years later, he and these other students are all still close friends, and he continues to actively participate in discussion groups as a way to be happily engaged with the world.

℞ FOR DEVELOPING YOUR BEST SELF

Are you ambitious? If not, why not? Could you aim higher? What would a realized ambition look like for you? Having the best class, best professors, best clubs, best friends, best internships, best junior year abroad, best major? Best degrees? You can make it happen now. If you don't have any ideas, ask around to get yourself started. Your goal is to turn college into your own personal laboratory, so that you can discover your own motivations and skills. It's the place where you can choose the most appropriate work to make a difference to the world and to your own life.

Chapter 5
Finding a Career—
No Matter Your Major

Don't aim at success—the more you aim at it and make it a target, the more you are going to miss it. For success, like happiness, cannot be pursued; it must ensue, and it only does so as the unintended side-effect of one's personal dedication to a cause greater than oneself or as the by-product of one's surrender to a person other than oneself.

—Victor Frankl

You hope that college will lead you somewhere. More than 90% of students think that "somewhere" means a great job—work that you do after you graduate to earn your living. Funny phrase, isn't it, "earning your living"? Since you have to do that, choose work in areas you are interested in, or chose fields you would be proud to be a part of—and start!

MAJOR CHOICES

Professional Majors Leading to a Career

Declaring a major is a major decision, indeed. It should be the indicator of where you'd like to go, but you'll know better only if you have real information. You can try several sources. For the most focused majors, such as accounting or engineering, you might get the best advice by interviewing successful accountants or engineers who can share what their working lives are really like. Top accountants, usually partners of firms, have had to learn along the way how to generate business. Talk to analysts for a specific industry. Find those who specialize in a field they wish they could be in—for example, by managing the finances of athletes, musicians, or physicians.

Or, if you choose engineering, learn the range of fields before you make a specific choice. Interview engineers who will tell you about their work. The career paths of some engineers show a surprising turn of events: they start out working on a team, but once they get promoted, they manage projects. If they continue to succeed and advance, they move up to more managerial roles and, ironically, no longer use the technical knowledge that was so important at the start of their careers. Sometimes engineers find they do not like, or feel suited for, the initial detailed work. If they prefer working with people, they might move to sales, where they interact with customers, resolve dilemmas, and promote their products. As they grow more successful, their commissions and bonuses increase. Many engineers continue with purely technical careers and are very successful. Be inspired by their stories as you find your own way.

Sometimes engineers, like others in other fields, find that they are not really interested in their first career choice. The smart thing to do is admit it early and choose again, this time more closely matching your interests to your work. There are many success stories of engineers who went back to graduate school to become doctors, lawyers, or mathematicians. If you pay attention to yourself, you can hone your interests as you go along.

Other Majors

The above are examples of the choices and dilemmas of many who make preprofessional and technical career decisions. But many of you are choosing less specific majors. What are you supposed to do with a degree in history, communications, political science, women's studies, or Latin or Asian studies? Liberal arts majors are not listed at career centers on job listing sites. Alas, you will not see a special booth for these majors at job fairs, nor will you see one for all the engineering or accounting jobs. It's hard to choose between finance and economics or between sociology and psychology, for example. No doubt about it, choosing is hard. But know that your choice does not exclude everything else.

Don't be afraid you will be stuck without a path to a career; quite the contrary. The good news is that employers, including software companies and financial firms, tell me that they prefer to hire graduates who have developed critical skills in thinking, speaking, and writing. Even recruiters for the best accounting firms say that they are primarily searching for students whom they can trust to communicate effectively with their clients. Employers reveal that they can train you to do almost any job; they just need you to come with demonstrated intelligence, dedication, and curiosity. Employers mostly need generalists who can search out answers, solve problems without detailed instructions, and supplement their software with brainpower. Ultimately, they want people with the ability to draw on the past and present in order to shape the future.

This is where you can shine. Make the following your mantra as you plan your work life:

I went to college because I enjoy the discipline of thinking creatively and critically. I am interested in

The World Future Society—a Washington, DC based professional association and clearinghouse for ideas and forecasts about the future—predicts the following career opportunities over the next 10–25 years:

- *Artificial intelligence technician*
- *Aquaculturist*
- *Automotive fuel cell battery technician*
- *Benefits analyst*
- *Bionic medical technician*
- *Computational linguist*
- *Computer microprocessor technician*
- *Cryonics technician*
- *Electronic mail technician*
- *Fiber optic technician*
- *Fusion engineer*
- *Horticulture therapist*
- *Image consultant*
- *Information broker*
- *Information center manager*
- *Job developer*
- *Leisure consultant*
- *Materials utilization specialist*
- *Medical diagnostic imaging technician*
- *Myotherapist*
- *Relocation counselor*
- *Retirement counselor*
- *Robot technician*
- *Shyness consultant*
- *Software club director*
- *Space mechanic*
- *Underwater archaeologist*
- *Water quality specialist*

researching trends and data and presenting ideas clearly. My major (from arts to science) has also made me engage in critical thinking. My thoughts may open up vistas of more thoughts. My choice of major indicates that I get excited about intellectual, scientific, or arts-related discussions. I enjoy the life of the mind. I'm in college for an excellent reason: knowledge for its own sake. I will be an asset to employers who need people who are willing to learn and keep learning.

Your major can help you narrow the field but not necessarily limit it.

THE LIBERAL ARTS MAJOR AS A JUMPING-OFF PLACE

Where are the jobs for liberal arts and humanities majors? Anywhere and everywhere. A cornucopia of job possibilities can be found in many different places. Here are some of the areas you can explore.

Advertising and public relations

- Writing liner notes for CDs
- Speechwriting for politicians or other officers (from colleges to corporations)
- Providing public relations support for new products
- Taking polls
- Managing accounts or clients
- Acting as an agent for clients in sports, entertainment, the arts, or cause-driven groups
- Consulting

Marketing and sales

- Conducting focus groups
- Researching future trends (from aging to toys to food fads)
- Developing strategic plans for Web sites
- Selling a variety of items for auctions, either in person or online

Media, technology, and the arts

- Writing interactive content
- Designing computer interfaces
- Working with computer software
- Processing data
- Composing jingles
- Writing copy for the Web

Education

- Teaching at private or public schools, community colleges, or universities

Finance and law

- Public accounting
- Working in investment and commercial banking
- Providing legal services

Ask alumni who have graduated from your college with your major what they did, and follow their advice and leads.

> *A new consulting business of dream architects to help people implement their dreams will show up.*
> —*Faith Popcorn*

Who Hires Liberal Arts Grads?

The answer is: all types of employers. Some companies even prefer that you have not yet settled on your career. They want to train and mold you, and then place you where you can contribute most effectively. Liberal arts graduates frequently find jobs in the following areas: sales, management, training, public relations, client relations, human relations, customer service, technical writing, and paralegal, health, and arts services. These opportunities exist within the majority of sizeable organizations, whether they make soap or airplanes or serve clients or countries. Here is a partial list of job specialties:

- Communication services
- Consulting services
- Hospitality (airlines, hotel, tours, travel)
- Computer software/data processing and finance
- Teaching
- Merchandising (buying, management, retail)
- Government (local, state, federal)
- Finance and banking (analysis, management, public relations, recruiting)
- Commercial banking—corporate, government, and public affairs; lending, management
- Insurance
- Advertising

- Marketing
- Legal services
- Business services (health, science, arts)
- Real estate
- Management
- Technical writing and editing
- Public relations
- Contract and grant writing

Of course, no one can predict or anticipate every detail of the future. As one industry emerges, it might overtake or explode an existing industry. With the rise of computers one might have predicted the demise of the world of paper, pens, and pencils. Instead, growth in the computer industry spurred new opportunities for output of print media, created new demands for record keeping, and laid the foundation for an explosion in creative output.

As a liberal arts major, you are eligible for the existing three sectors in the marketplace: the for-profit business world, the nonprofit world, and government work. Learn about each before you make your selection. You might be surprised to find out how each is growing rapidly and requires new skill sets, which gives you a distinct advantage.

If your mission is to do well by doing good, you could be part of the exciting world of social entrepreneurship. People who can combine social skills with generalized knowledge are needed to fill a wide range of new careers in nonprofit management and philanthropy for which there are now courses, certificates, and even doctoral programs. You can be part of a fast-growing career track just when you are starting out. You might choose to work for the growing group of profit-making organizations committed to contributing to the well-being of society. In this highly entrepreneurial age, when initiative and multitasking are eagerly sought after, you can play to your strengths.

> *It seems clear that when students perceive that they are free to follow their own goals, most of them invest more of themselves in their effort, work harder, and retain and use more of what they have learned.*
> —*Carl Rogers*

Career Strategies for Liberal Arts Majors

Because there is often no direct path to your goal, the possibilities are limitless. Therefore, I suggest the following steps:

1. Join student activities to meet people and to build your team-work and leadership skills.
2. Get feedback and referrals from professors, and turn them into mentors.
3. Become familiar with major categories of software, including operating systems, word processors, spreadsheets, Web browsers, and photo editors.
4. Research Web sites of organizations that interest you to see their growth potential.
5. Explore internships in nonprofits such as city government agencies, cause-related groups, from the United Way to United Cerebral Palsy, as well as small or large for-profit companies, technical and professional firms, such as Arthur Anderson or McKinsey, and arts organizations, such as the Getty.
6. Take a job with a promising company and, in a year or so, work your way in and up, cross training to find more compelling work.
7. Work on campus and learn the great variety of jobs, from teaching to administration, from faculty to student affairs, from university relations to fundraising.
8. Interview and/or work for entrepreneurs or solo practitioners in fields that sound interesting to you, whether it's law, catering, or animal services.
9. Research graduate programs that might offer fellowships or ventures in professions, arts, and business.
10. Go to your university's career center for workshops, feedback, tips, internship leads, and jobs. Studies prove that students who take advantage of this free service actually find better jobs at higher pay with greater satisfaction than those who don't (see Chapter 9).
11. Pay attention to professors and employers who might play important roles in your career. They can mentor you and may become partners in a future venture.
12. Develop strategies by telling your professors, family, and interviewers what you really can do: write, research on the computer, plan events, do fundraising. Point out the skills you've developed and what you want to do, even if you're not sure. It is a starting point. After all, you must start somewhere, or nothing can happen.
13. Describe your specific goals and specific skills to employers or to temporary agencies hired to outsource entry and/or technical

skills. Do this even if you think you'll change your goals, as you probably will, maybe several times.

14. Do not depend on landing a job by sending out dozens of résumés, whether by regular mail or e-mail. You still have to call and demonstrate why you should be hired. You need to prove your experience by describing your activities, internships, and part-time jobs. If you have not done these things before, pursue them now!

15. Remember that a particular job offer goes to the best job searcher and best interviewee. Your intelligence is not the only factor; the smartest person who applies doesn't necessarily get the job. Landing a job takes concentrated effort. Your success will depend on developing job search skills and finding the determination to go through the process.

You may know what your career should be, or you might not have a clue. Most of us don't know. You will find out only by trying new things and following where your instincts and opportunities lead.

Internships for Liberal Arts Majors

Internships provide a foot in the door and a competitive advantage. Here are the stories of some liberal arts majors who took their chances and signed up for internships.

Barry, a communications major, was planning on a career in human resources (HR) because he liked people. After an internship spent crunching numbers and filing forms, Barry discovered that HR was the wrong choice. He was disappointed but grateful that he found out in time to search for something he liked more.

Joe, a senior in urban planning, couldn't find an internship that suited him, so he designed his own. He asked if he could work for the government of small city near the university. The planning department was receptive. As an intern, Joe did even more than he was asked to do. When he graduated, he applied for a full-time job in the planning department. They did not have one to offer, so he asked for a job in another department until one opened up. Today, Joe is the head of that city's planning department.

A television major, Laurel knew that she would need an internship to get her foot in the door of the entertainment industry. That industry lets you earn academic credit in lieu of pay for the privilege of such access. But Laurel was disappointed that her internship was based only on menial tasks such as filing. Instead of throwing away her chances, as did her fellow interns, she not only did her job, but she did much more. She was enthusiastic about meeting people in the contracts office and found projects that she could work on. Because of her extra effort and obvious interest, Laurel was the only one of the six interns who was offered a paying job.

These interns' experiences are not unusual. Barry's story represents the worst that can happen: you discover that you don't like a particular field that you thought you did. I say, "Great!" Better to find out *now* that you don't like something so that you're more informed in a search for what you do like. Joe's story reveals that you are not limited by internships that already exist. Why not create your own? Laurel's story also demonstrates how internships really work. For you, internships are a way to test jobs and companies. In the same way, companies use internships to test you out. They want to hire those who are self-motivated, who pitch in instead of waiting around passively for an assignment. Sometimes companies will even hire interns and pay them a salary before their internship period ends.

Some students have derived an indirect benefit from their internships: networking that leads them to other places. One English major in Los Angeles took an internship with a small, active public relations firm nearby and got to work on the film *Blair Witch Project*. When his good work and healthy attitude became evident, his boss recommended him to another firm, where he was offered a full-time job. That, in turn, led him to an Internet job in New York. He took the chance and moved.

Only a small percentage of interns are actually offered jobs on site, so do not expect to be asked. But interns who work hard, contribute enthusiastically, and do more than they are asked impress their bosses, who can offer recommendations to colleagues in other firms if they can't hire the interns themselves.

Choosing Without Eliminating Everything Else

Start with what you love doing. That might be based on your major or on a cocurricular activity. Suppose you can write and you love entertainment or sports. Why not consider a talent agency or a public relations firm that handles clients from these fields? If you like research and would love to help the environment, you can combine these interests in a summer job or internship that will, in turn, lead you to a first job.

Visit your career center. It exists for the express purpose of directing and launching you. Make an appointment with a counselor with specialized knowledge in your major and talk over your best and worst subjects, your activities, and the roles you played in them. Ask for leads for internships, which are usually semester-long part-time jobs that are related to your interests. If you take to it, ask for a full-time job after graduation. Use the career center's job-listing service and recommended Web sites. Follow up on what looks interesting. Go to the job fairs on campus dressed in business attire with copies of your résumé in hand. Talk to all the recruiters from big and small companies at their booths. And don't forget to ask for leads from your best professors, counselors, coaches, and sponsors, who all have connections to the outside world.

Budda left a road map.
Jesus left a road map.
Kirshna left a road map.
Rand McNally left a road map.
But you still have to travel the
road yourself.
—Stephen Levine

GRADUATE SCHOOL

While graduate school, at both the master's and doctoral levels, used to be optional for entering a career, it is now required for many professions, including law, medicine, engineering, arts, psychology, accounting, and business. Nearly all humanities and English majors are acceptable to graduate schools for master's programs in business administration and public administration, as well as for certain related and vocational degrees. Usually you will have to pass the Graduate Record Exam (GRE) or other specialized admissions test.

You can either prepare while you are an undergraduate, or you can work for several years in order to save money and better evaluate your choices. For the most part, there is no penalty for taking your time. But don't take too much time, or you may lose out to your competitors. You might discover that you are a perennial student, one who wants a third or fourth degree. If you're a physician, you might move on to study law to become a forensic lawyer. If you're a lawyer with an engineering degree who likes technical work, you might choose patent law. The choices are endless; each one can change your life for good. Still, you have to decide. To decide wisely, you need information. Read catalogs, talk to professors, and interview accomplished people in your desired field. Take your pulse and choose what excites you.

Lifelong learning, once only a concept, is now the norm. It is not unusual for people to return for advanced degrees every 7 years to refocus their careers as they recharge their enthusiasm. There are many certificate programs as well as summer programs that provide expertise for the marketplace, as well as the sheer pleasure of learning. Use these resources well and enjoy them.

Because graduate school is expensive and demanding, it pays to be as focused as you can in determining what you really want to study. If you don't know what to study, take time out to explore. Join the Peace Corps or AmeriCorps, volunteer for a project, or take a corporate training program. Any of these will broaden your worldview and teach you about a range of options. But always forge connections between your program and your career prospects. Make sure that your papers and projects link you to your profession. Do some research about any graduate program; read catalogs and talk to professors and alumni. Your graduate program does not have to follow your undergraduate major. Many people change their minds as they change their worlds.

DO'S AND DON'TS FOR USING COLLEGE TO FIND YOUR LIFE'S DIRECTION

Don't: Take only safe subjects, settle for just good enough, or expect that your calling will come to you in a flash. Epiphanies are rare.

Do: Explore. Follow what interests you and identify and build on your passions. Don't try to get away with just the minimum; instead, take on meaningful projects with enthusiasm. Develop flexibility. Learn to perform on your own. Take chances to learn and grow with young companies, which will increase your value over time. By doing these things, you will discover skills and strengths that form a pattern. When you connect the dots of the pattern of your talents and interests, you will be on a path to job success and happiness. For example, if you find that you are interested in entertainment but can also understand its economy, you might become an investment analyst specializing in the industry, an information broker, or a Webcaster delivering customized information to a targeted client.

Don't: Expect that your career, once attained, will last forever.

Do: Expect surprises along the way. Here are some of the unexpected
         transformations that took place in the careers of some liberal
         arts majors with whom I've spoken recently:

- A psychology major became a bank recruiter.
- A geology student became a paleontologist working for an
  oil company.
- A history major became a fund-raiser for a medical school.
- A sociologist became president of a university.
- A graphic designer became a screenwriter.
- An architect became an events planner.
- A physician became a writer.
- A banker became a coffee broker.
- An engineer became a judge.
- A fashion designer became a concert pianist.
- A business manager became a popular lyricist.
- A spy became a movie star.
- A teacher became a health-food grocer.
- A minister became a career counselor.

FREQUENTLY ASKED QUESTIONS

*Q. I can't decide on a major, even though my friends have. I do not know what
I want to do with my life. How will I ever know?*

A. Knowing what to do with your life is a profound question. It's true that
some people do know, even at an early age, that they want to be a doctor, chef, or musician, but for the majority of others, the decision isn't
clear. There are an overwhelming number of choices and opportunities,
but don't let the numbers scare you. Make an appointment with your
career counselor and sign up for some workshops that will take you
through an exploration process to begin to identify your best subjects,
your interests, even your skills.

Most students choose a major because they are truly interested in the
subject. Some students are inspired by one professor, sign up for all his or
her courses, and major in it themselves. Others are guided by their families. Only a small percentage choose something just to be accepted to
college or simply guess at what might be appropriate. Another small percentage have not yet decided.

If you still cannot identify a major, then a vocational and personality test might offer you some starting points. Experiment—take electives that you might like, join clubs that call to you—and see what happens.

Q. *How can I make sure that my major is right for me?*

A. Here are five ways to start your search for your major and your career:

1. Ask professors in your best subjects if they think your major is right for you. Build a relationship with them beforehand so that they can see what your work is like and provide a real answer.

2. Use one of your assigned papers to explore your major. If you are assigned a political science paper, perhaps you can research your local office of a national party, the city council, or a public network. You will get involved and learn about a larger career (better or worse) than you would have imagined.

3   Find an internship or part-time job to get your feet wet in a field in which you are potentially interested. While you are there, ask about people's experiences and for their advice.

4   Join a club in your major subject and become active. Use the Journalism Club's program committee to question reporters or professionals about their careers; the Management Club's recruiters list for informational interviews; the Engineering Society for their networking evenings with professors and employers.

5   Take one or two of the vocational tests at your career center. Review your results with your counselor and use this as a Geiger counter—a starting point to lead you toward a career or away from one.

Q. *How do I network?*

A. You are just beginning the lifelong process of connecting to people. Networking is often misunderstood. It means much more than just being introduced and exchanging cards. It requires some relationship based on something you share—an interest in work, or politics, or arts, or religion. Not as personal as being friends, it is a friendly and reciprocal relationship with a genuine give-and-take of advice, leads, and support.

Creating one or more networks must become a regular part of your job search; it will be required for keeping your job once you get it. Start by talking to everyone you meet as if you were at a party. Play the role of host even if you're not the host. Get out of the habit of being the passive guest waiting around for introductions and expecting invitations.

When you join a professional club and volunteer for one of its projects or committees, understand that part of the reason for doing this unpaid work is the chance to meet and bond with classmates and employers. Learn to talk to them; ask questions about how they got started, what they like doing, what they did versus what they do now.

Keep a record of whom you have met, what they are like, what you asked of them, what you promised to send. And always thank people for their time and help—in person or by phone, note, or e-mail.

Q. I am returning to college with a full-time job and a husband, who is also a student. I need time to study, but my husband doesn't get it. I end up feeling guilty. Any suggestions?

A. This is a resolvable dilemma that many women share. Because you want to study, it is up to you to take the initiative to work out a different plan with your husband. Think more like a change agent. It is not his job to suggest it; it is yours. Create a schedule for the next week and ask him to stipulate which hours of which days he would like to devote to work and which to study. Mark them down in one color ink, then you do the same in red ink. Schedule grocery shopping, cleaning, and any other chores, then split them up.

You do deserve time to study without feeling guilty. When you take time, mark it well. Seclude yourself either by closing your door and putting a "Do Not Disturb" sign on it or by going to the library. Do the same for him. Expect the same respect back or you will never get it. You can build a much more loving and cooperative marriage based on what you agree to do right now.

Help yourselves along in this process by setting aside twenty minutes for each other every night. Divide the time in half—ten minutes each—so that you can take turns sharing your separate activities. Set rules; do not complain. Do not settle for worse behavior from each other than you would tolerate at work or in class. Make a pact to include time to tell why you love each other. And be dedicated in this activity. Do not let this shared time disappear as your semester's schedules pile up.

Q. I am just finishing my Associate Arts degree at my neighborhood community college and I wonder where to transfer. My parents want me to stay close and choose the local state college, but I want to go north to a women's college, even though I am not sure I could get in or do well. How do I get my parents to let me go?

A. You are on the right track! Most women's colleges have much higher expectations for their students than coed colleges. Look at their Web sites and apply. More than 50% of students at women's colleges receive financial aid, so do not be too timid to ask. When you graduate, your salary will no doubt be higher than a coed graduate, which means you can pay back any loans you take. Make your case to your parents: tell them that women do better, choose better, are safer, aim higher, have better marriages and careers, and feel better at women's colleges. Studies show that women are grateful to their college and remain active throughout their lives as mentors, employers, and even trustees.

Here's a role model for you: Leslie Stahl, CBS's 60 *Minutes* correspondent. She found her career in television journalism directly through her experience at a women's college. Her male professors dedicated themselves to training students to debate men and believed women could achieve anything they wanted. Her advisors for her thesis on how World War II actually started were considerably helpful in leading her to identify the human, rather than economic, factors.

Chapter 6
Gaining Internships, Working, Service Learning, and Volunteering

All our dreams can come true if we have the courage to pursue them.
—Walt Disney

THE VALUE OF GETTING INVOLVED

If I could, I would require every student in every major to take as many work and volunteer experiences as possible before graduating. It is only through these kinds of experiences, which you yourself choose, that you learn more about who you are now and who you want to be. It is particularly valuable to see your story and dreams compared to your classmates with very different experiences and backgrounds. Never before has a college campus been such a world microcosm with immigrant and foreign students and with those from different races, religions, and economic backgrounds—all with different ideas, values, and histories. College is often your first chance to find friends from a more diverse student body than you ever imagined. You will come to care about classmates whom you may have met through work in a soup kitchen, a cancer walk, a work-study assignment in the student activities office, or an internship for a biotech company or investment firm. This will enrich your view of the world and increase your chance to make a difference.

Search out these opportunities, drop in, and sign up for those that interest you. You may find, as many other students have, how to make college a richer experience. Your major may not turn out to be the only important factor in your career decision as you find other experiences that might be even better suited to your skills and interests.

Sarah's Story: A Volunteer Finds a Home

We do not always know what we are interested in. Interests need to be uncovered and explored. Here is the story of a student who used an internship to explore an unfamiliar area that had piqued her curiosity.

An environmental geography major, Sarah worked part time in her university's law library to help pay her tuition. Without feeling much passion for either her courses or her work, she decided to try an internship in an area she had just read about with a bit of interest. During her duties at the city planning council meetings, Sarah discovered that she had "come home," experiencing a great sense of belonging. She redirected her major, throwing herself into her studies. Not only did Sarah create her own internship, she also began the more significant task of reshaping herself.

Note that Sarah did not just walk in and get assigned to the most interesting project with the most visibility—not by a long shot. Initially, she performed menial "gofer" tasks: answering phones, stuffing envelopes, clipping newspaper stories, and proofreading papers. She had to learn to forgo her ego and act willing, even eager, to perform without complaint. In addition to her involvement in her work, she had a chance to advance in her course of study and gain perspective on how an office actually works. She also had the unique advantage of observing role models and work possibilities right under her nose. Here she was part of things, working alongside some of the people she most admired, on projects with which she was becoming fascinated. She made time to ask the planners about their career stories and personal goals, such as how they began and why they continued. What could be more rewarding and worth the risk?

INTERNSHIPS: TEST-DRIVE YOUR CAREER

Internships are a real-world, practical complement to classroom theory. They act as the bridge between college and a full-time position after graduation. Your sense of how to choose for yourself becomes stronger as you increase your options. Finding learning experiences outside of college, while you're enrolled, whether paid positions or not, provides a great perspective from which to find out more about what exists in the world and where your own longings lie. Matching your talents to your real-world interests is one of the challenges of college. Practical experiences provide the opportunity to learn more about an industry, a company, or a particular special interest that will help you determine where to begin to identify your career.

Surveys show that more than one-third of students who intern at organizations are hired by the employer after graduation, and half of all new hires had previous internship experience. You will be more competitive with this experience, which is gaining in importance each year. Internships offer a great range in salary—from nom pay to high pay. But whether paid in money or in credits, you'll have a chance to experience an organization firsthand, determine whether you enjoy its work, possibly find a career "home" for yourself, and if so, land a part-time job now and a full-time job after graduation. Check out the list of internships for the best value—quality companies you'd like to work for, the perks that they offer, and the chance to connect with the company and other interns. Typically months long, internships in the top Fortune 500 companies, like Microsoft, McKinsey, or Procter & Gamble, or in government or the arts, such as the White House or the Getty, offer special programs.

Even those that start with fairly menial tasks can offer you insight. You are likely to be assigned a "gofer" role, running errands and performing small necessary tasks for anyone who needs something done. Sometimes you are assigned to assist someone who might be working on a special project. Being assigned a "floating" position gives you a snapshot of what goes on within the organization and the chance to make connections with many different people.

Mailroom duty has been legendary in the entertainment industry. Being assigned to deliver mail to agents or movie and television studio executives, a seemingly low-level internship, has catapulted many to jobs inside an otherwise closed, entrepreneurial industry. You can just deliver mail or you can use that assignment to learn the structure of the organization and its functions. You can just deliver mail or you can connect to people and areas that appeal to you and offer to help above and beyond your assignment. The assignment itself is a test to see if you have what it takes to succeed. This not-so-subtle *attitude* (not *aptitude*) test is so powerfully important that a few studios have a policy of limiting their employment of inexperienced people in the mailroom for only six months with the proviso that if you cannot make a connection within that time, then you are probably not suited to this kind of work, which is so heavily dependent on transactional behavior. If you are suited to it, an internship provides the most direct means of access to a job within this high-demand industry.

On the other hand, landing a *specific* assignment gives you direct experience in learning both the rewards and difficulties of working with a team. You become better known to the people with whom you work because the group is smaller. Either way, students report that internships are the very best way to find out what goes on and find whether or not it is right for you. If it is, you get the edge on a potential job; if not, you know to change directions. Your future begins with the links you forge now. Internships provide so much—experience, connections, and fun.

A prelaw major found an internship in a law firm as a paralegal. However, he found he disliked the work so much that he changed his major. Another student in the same internship program found it to be her calling. The firm was so pleased with her work that she was hired on part time and during summers; they helped her apply to her mentor's law school, and she was accepted. Which of these outcomes is better? Neither; both interns were steered into something good for them. Only through applied work and experience "in the trenches" can you decide what is best for you.

Internships are not a new idea. In fact, the oldest and most traditional internship program is in physician training, where year-long internships follow immediately after four years of medical study as a prerequisite to becoming licensed. In law school, between the second and third years, students typically take summer internships with firms they hope to join. Like graduate medical students, law students have to be aggressive to land such internships. If they succeed, they are frequently offered positions with that firm following graduation. Some law graduates go on to clerk for judges in a more formal system of internship. In education, there is a long internship history called "student teaching," which is helpful both for practicing your chosen profession and judging whether or not your choice is appropriate for you.

Business organizations are now increasingly following suit by offering more internships to students. Accounting firms, technology and aerospace firms, and manufacturing and oil companies find this is a good way to identify potential talent and to establish a reservoir of qualified future employees before beginning the expensive process of hiring them. Businesses also hope that students will bring them the latest academic theory and technology. Student interns must quickly learn to pitch in and go that extra mile in a work environment with intense daily pressures and chaotic work schedules. Everyone thinks it is well worth it. Don't be left out.

Internships can also act as a bridge of time between college semesters and employers' hiring needs. Consider the plight of Sheila, an accounting major who graduated in January but was not able to be hired by a top accounting firm until June. When Sheila asked her career counselor how she could best spend the upcoming five months, she was directed to an accounting internship at Disney, complete with a formal orientation program. It gave her direct experience in licensing products, a valuable experience for the accounting firm, which she joined in June. She did more than just hang around for six months: she took the chance, learned a great deal, and moved on to her targeted firm ahead of others.

Work-study programs were pioneered by the University of Cincinnati, Antioch College, and Philadelphia's Drexel University, where students were required to find paid jobs in their areas of study for academic credit as part of the academic curriculum. Smith College's model internship program offers hundreds of opportunities for their liberal arts undergraduate women. California colleges and universities have participated in the Educational Participation in Communities (EPIC) program, which offers students real-life work experience to help them develop job skills and explore career options, while at the same time helping them to solve problems in the community.

Internships continue to grow in number and in opportunity. I wish I could require you to take one or two. You are never taught how to be assertive in college, but you do have to find an experience that allows you to practice, even if it is uncomfortable at first. Your future depends on it. If your career center doesn't have an internship program, or if you can't find an internship that you really want, ask a career counselor or internship coordinator to help you create one. But if they cannot, do not let that stop you. You can always initiate your own internship. Here's how:

- Find an organization for which you think you would like to work.
- Decide on the department in which you would like to work or plan to rotate among several different departments to find which you prefer.
- Call the department(s) in which you are interested and offer yourself as an intern, even if they do not have an established program.

Do not overlook your professors, who are often consultants to companies within your areas of interest. They are likely to have direct contacts and networks of associates to get you started. Learn the process of thanking everyone who has helped you, and stay in contact with them by giving regular progress reports and asking for feedback or advice. Call or e-mail. Informing others of your progress and expressing appreciation for their support is what establishes a healthy mentor-protégé relationship.

Q: What is the real job of an internship?

  a.   To fulfill the requirements and tasks as well as possible
  b.   To test out how you fit in the company or industry
  c.   To try to anticipate what is necessary rather than wait for an assignment
  d.   To connect with at least one person who will make you a job offer and/or write you a letter of recommendation

A: All of the above.
  What do you get as an intern? A chance to:

- see first-hand the work that you have only imagined;
- see if it works for you;
- put what you've been studying to work;
- experience a new world of people from different races, cultures, classes, jobs, and abilities, all working together;
- roll up your sleeves and make yourself think problems through;
- experience a full day's work;
- observe an organization's culture; and
- build a network of people to whom you can connect now and in the future.

Using Internships as Direction Finders

If you do not have a clear notion of what you want to do following graduation, you are not alone. This is true of more students than ever! If you are looking for direction, an internship can help clarify your uncertainties and focus your interests. Which organizations should you consider? The answer, of course, is all kinds: newspapers, hospitals, radio and television stations, emergency help centers, political organizations, religious groups, retail stores, import-export businesses, libraries, research labs, schools, advertising and public relations agencies, factories, labor unions, and financial firms. In short, you should consider all kinds of small and large businesses, arts organizations, services, and professions. Choose the one closest to your own interests and course of study, and go exploring.

After Cal State Northridge students finish their internships—from entertainment to biotech to insurance—their accounts of their internships are videotaped by the career center. Here are some of their self-reports following their internships:

- "I found myself."
- "I discovered a whole world that I never knew about."
- "I found the biotech company that was the most alive I could ever imagine."
- "I was so happy to be in the movie industry with a chance to belong; I'd never get there on my own."
- "I saw people working together on a campaign to really make a difference, which made me want to join them. I never felt so much a part of something."
- "I became part of a team under a brilliant leader and did more than I had ever done in my life."

The following are eight questions you should ask yourself after your internship:

1. Did it meet your expectations? If not, why not?
2. Did you talk to your employers and find out what they expected of you? If not, what else could you have done?
3. When you met difficulties, did you ask for help?
4. Did you ever ask for feedback about how you were doing?
5. Did you talk to the employees about their work, their lives, and their goals?
6. Did you make yourself valuable and likeable?
7. Do you still want to work for that company or any other in the industry? If so, did you ask for the job and promise to stay in touch?
8. If you did not like what you experienced, did you get yourself a second internship to find your dream job?

As a college student, how do you make your first career choices? Too often students are programmed to pursue what is currently trendy. I can usually tell the decade in which people went to college by their majors. Looking back over the past fifty years, it is easy to spot the hot majors. In the 1950s, men went to college to become engineers and women to become teachers. In the 1960s, men studied community service or psychology, while women pursued social work or sociology. In the 1970s, men went to school for computer science or law; women began to study law or entered MBA programs. By the 1980s, business became the most common major for both genders. In the 1990s, the most popular major, communications, strongly attracted both men and women. Even though the number of women students now outnumbers men, journalism jobs are still predominantly male. In the 2000s, the trendy jobs of accounting and communications have attracted both sexes.

You cannot escape the fact that individuals live among trends. The dilemma has always been to choose wisely yet personally among a wide range of choices. There is a heavy cost in not bringing your own desires into the career equation. Too many students come out of school understimulated, dissatisfied, and still undecided about what to do with their degrees. Why? Because their choices were not based on their own personal strengths and interests. Where do you discover information about how to choose your life's work? TV shows and movies feed society caricatured images of medicine, law, media, and police work. This, alas, is all many people know about certain jobs.

You are in the position of choosing a career without having much experience on which to base it. Like that old line about understanding art, that you will "know it when you see it," students expect the same of their best career choice; yet you can't usually pull a career out of thin air, even if you do recognize your own talents and preferences. However, you can use your time in college to experiment with ideas and possibilities, including courses, professors, internships, and jobs, to find your calling— the work you are best suited to do.

Some words of comfort: People who do not know what they want to do are not idiots. A UCLA survey found differences between those female students who came to college with preset career goals and majors and those who were undecided. The undecided students tested as more intelligent and flexible, finally making appropriate choices after a process of trial and error. So don't worry too much if, at first, you don't know what you want to do. Finding your interests is your college assignment. The more you experience, the greater your chances of finding what really suits you.

Intern #1: Fine-Tuning

An internship gives you the chance to test your plans. If you enjoy it, you can start to build a network of people in the field. If you don't, you have time to explore other options before you graduate. It is a low-risk venture, which may lead to your dream job.

One intern found a career that suited him even better than the dream job he originally imagined. From the first time he listened to music on the radio, Gary had wanted to be a disc jockey. It seemed to him that DJs were powerful people who had the best job in the world. His dreams came true in college when he landed an internship with a local radio show that played top-40 hits. However, as an intern, he was required to perform a variety of tasks that were quite different from the job of DJ: delivering the mail, running errands, helping on a promotional campaign, and substituting for a vacationing salesperson. He discovered, to his astonishment, that these other jobs were not only significant, but that marketing and sales were his real talents. Redirecting his childhood dream, he developed a successful career in media marketing. Taking the slight risk of interning at a radio station, Gary learned about areas that he would not have thought of before. This internship was his "direction finder." Today he is the president of a major network.

Intern #2: Shifting Gears

Here's another kind of internship experience; this one reveals how wrong a career choice can be.

Richard had always wanted to be a teacher. Near the end of his college program, he signed up for student teaching, the traditional internship in the education field. He was assigned to teach history in a public high school. Midway through the semester, Richard realized that he had made a bad choice for himself. It was history itself that he loved, not the actual teaching process. He did not have enough patience for his students, he disliked the slow pace of teaching, and he felt constrained by the restrictions in text selection. At the end of student teaching, he shifted gears. He found another internship at the city newspaper. Because of his teaching experience, they accepted his proposal for a special series on education. During his time at the paper, he sought out news reporters for advice and was hired by one of those reporters, who had been promoted to editor. Two attempts gave Richard the chance to know himself more clearly so that he could identify his own interests and style. His courage to change served him in the very best way.

Intern #3: A Psych Experiment That Paid Off

Lisa's is another internship account about second thoughts. She had chosen psychology as an undergraduate major but was disappointed when classroom theory didn't match her fantasy of the drama of psychotherapy.

As a last chance to test herself before she changed majors, Lisa interned at a local crisis clinic, taking incoming calls on the hotline. After she proved herself able, she was invited to assist a group counselor, and finally trained to be a lay therapist. By the time she graduated, she had a caseload of her own clients. Lisa's internship served to affirm her original choice and saved her career. This intervention also taught her about the nature of experimenting. She is a much better therapist now than she would ever have been without the internship experience.

Some colleges are trying to forge the connection between students and alumni who have the same career interests. Through shared career experiences and professional insights over lunch or dinner, the students get an up-close, personal view of a profession. They can see the advantages and disadvantages, check their assumptions, and whet their appetites. This process allows them to sort out previously held choices or decide to pursue others. If your college has student-alumni connection activities, be sure to find out about them and sign up.

Be Someone Else for a Day

I managed a yearlong interactive conference whose purpose was to provide career reality checks. Called "Alternative Pursuits to America's Third Century," the conference helped participants from all walks of life and from all over the country to plan and implement their own community service. Before attendees were allowed to create an original career design, they had to "be someone else for a day." This exercise required conferees to pick several careers that interested them, no matter how unrealistic these choices were. Then they had to find people who worked in those fields, follow them around, and observe closely what they actually did during the course of a full day.

This experiment thoroughly shattered these participants' illusions. I remember one psychologist who had thought that investigative reporting would be the most stimulating job imaginable. Feeling his own career choice too safe and slow in delivering results, he found, to his amazement, that the actual work of tracking down clues was completely boring to him and an ultimately unrewarding process. He was able to reassess what he was doing and revised his advice to his own patients to reflect what he had learned about the dangers of defining one's vocation on the basis of fantasy without checking it out first. He became far more stimulated and more effective in finding keys to his patients' dilemmas.

Another participant, a social worker, took the opposite route and chose what she thought was the worst occupation, namely as a waitress. Going to a local diner to observe the waitress's routine, she discovered that her subject did much more than just take orders and bring the food. Under close observation, waitresses turned out to be on-the-spot social workers, joking easily with regular customers, asking about their lives, sympathizing with their problems, and celebrating their progress. It was a revelation to this professional woman, who had considered her own job the ultimate helping profession. She came away with a completely new perspective on the social nature of work.

Imagine what field you'd choose, how you could observe as a "fly on the wall," and how your observations might match your fantasies.

Internship Do's and Don'ts

An internship can offer many rich opportunities, but don't expect miracles. Don't complain if you feel that your assigned task is beneath you, if you are not appreciated, if the work is too complicated for a minimal or nonexistent wage, or if the assignment is too chaotic or meaningless. If your assigned work isn't going well, don't ignore it, try to fudge it, or wait for someone to come rescue you. Ask for help from your supervisor. You are not expected to know the ropes, but you are expected to be honest and responsible. Getting advice when you need it is part of the job.

Take it as it comes. Be enthusiastic, friendly, and ready to help. Don't take obvious sides in office politics. Save your personal questions for casual, off-work times, such as lunch or breaks. Don't ask for career advice too often from your coworkers, but do ask which courses might provide good background for your field, which to skip, how to gain entry to your chosen career, and finally, what to consider in choosing a career. Ask your supervisors for stories about their professional experiences, so that you can gain insight into the nature of this kind of work. When you don't know what to do next, ask. You will not only be learning how to get along with people in an office situation, but you will also be increasing your awareness of your field. Such an opportunity can turn the job into the beneficial experience it could be.

Internship Strategies

Sign up for one internship each semester. Find a list of internships at your career center or online. You can also create your own. Internships give you an entrée to the work you may secretly desire to explore, ranging from for-profit corporations to nonprofits such as education, research, politics, and government.

Tip #1: Don't expect organizations to give you a course outline. The real world does not work in that organized way of focusing on your best interests. Instead, do everything they ask and more. Inquire, find out what people are doing, offer your assistance, and you will be included in groups that interest you.

Here's how to start:

- Research the companies and industries you find interesting.
- Have an updated résumé.
- Write a basic cover letter to which you add the new company name and contact name for each use.
- Lead with a brief first paragraph explaining why you would be perfect for that internship or job.
- Interview for it, but learn how first!
- Dress the part.
- Follow up with a thank you note and phone calls so the interviewers remember you.

Tip #2: Act like a talk show host in your daily life—interview everyone you meet. Imagine you have your own talk show, and everyone is your guest: faculty, school staff, coworkers, and bosses. Ask questions. As a talk show host, your script might include a list of questions like these:

- How did you get started?
- What do you like about your job?
- What is the hardest part of your job?
- What have been the greatest surprises?
- What kind of help did you get along the way?
- How did you get this job?
- What advice do you have for me?

By the way, don't worry about being a pest; people relish talking about themselves. And when it is your turn to help a student, you will do the same.

Work is less boring than amusing oneself.
—Charles Baudelaire

WORKING YOUR WAY THROUGH

Work in any form offers extraordinary possibilities to further your education and connections. You can and should profit from it,

The Twelve Best Reasons to Work

1. *Work provides active, hands-on experience—often a welcome change from sitting in class taking notes.*
2. *Work will make you feel more like an adult and less like a dependent student.*
3. *Work reinforces your ego as you switch roles from anxious test-taker to eager doer. This is particularly true for older, returning students who are accustomed to autonomy and responsibility.*
4. *Work helps confirm a career decision; the prospect of working will speed you on to get hired.*
5. *Work can confirm when a career decision is not appropriate for you, and can act as a catalyst to redirect you.*
6. *Work provides a laboratory in which to test theories learned in class, and it presents situations in which you can practice solving real problems.*
7. *Work offers opportunities to bring experience to bear on class-room work, thereby enriching it.*
8. *Work helps you develop the critical interpersonal skills of communication and collaboration.*
9. *Work helps pay for tuition and living expenses.*
10. *Work serves as a transitional bridge between college and career.*
11. *Work provides the gratification of problem-solving and working on projects in the real world.*
12. *Ultimately, work can connect you to your spirit and transform your life.*

whether it is on campus or off, full time or part time, work-study or a paid or unpaid internship. The only drawback is that work is time-consuming and energy-consuming. You will have to develop your time-management skills and budget your time for both study and social activities. Forget about relaxing.

If you are smart and lucky, you can match your work to your existing interests. It is worth sacrificing to find that appropriate work. If you are interested in the entertainment field, which traditionally does not pay its interns, go after that internship anyway to gain entrance, even if it means having to take a paying job at night or over the weekends.

Work serves several purposes. You can achieve its benefits if you use work for more than just earning money. Students who work at part-time or summer jobs just to pay expenses often live in a double world and do not make the best use of college. To make both work and life better, look for jobs that interest you and enhance your experiences, or find a way to make a dull job more interesting.

A district attorney who had never lost a case told me a story from his past, a story that became a touchstone for his later success. To supplement a partial college scholarship, he worked as a salesclerk in a department store. Bored, he decided to experiment to see if he could differentiate those customers who would buy something from those who were just browsing. When he acquired this skill, he stepped up his experiment: he tried to sell to the nonbuyers. In the process, he taught himself the psychology of sales, motivation, and persuasion—skills that he further developed as a trial lawyer, successfully winning over to his side every judge and jury.

Think of it. Whether you work in a jeans store, the university's fundraising office, or the sales department in a TV station, you have a rich experimental field before you. It is ripe for anything you want to study or have been assigned. Our district attorney could have continued his experiment and written up his findings for papers in psychology or business courses, as well as in the campus newspaper, a marketing journal, or even the local newspaper's business section. What he learned enriched and emboldened him, and it paid his living expenses.

The Ten Worst Reasons to Work

1. You want an expensive apartment without the bother of roommates.
2. You want a new car now and don't want the hassle of the old one.
3. You want a social life.
4. You want to buy prepared food and coffee instead of making your own.
5. You do not want to search for a scholarship or student loan.
6. You do not know what else to do with your spare time.
7. You spend too much money on gifts for others.
8. All your friends work, and you want to keep up.
9. You have to pay off credit card debt for the clothes and other things you bought without admitting that you'd have to pay later.
10. Your job is dead-end, offers minimum wage, and is almost begging you to find something better.

A graduate student confided to me that her part-time job was delivering beer to students on campus. She said it was a waste of her time. I asked if she was interested in the beverage profession, either breweries, microbreweries, or wines. There could be a career lurking there. For example, she might interview the top salesman and saleswoman to see what their careers are really like. I asked if students would buy anything else, like chips, cookies, or sandwiches. If so, she could bring in more business or create one of her own. If she wasn't interested in any of this, she should find another job and make better use of her time to benefit herself.

Expanding your job is totally up to you. Probably no one will tell you how, but if you take the initiative, your momentum can carry other people along with you, which is a valuable lesson as you go through life. If you recognize your own entrepreneurial interests, plan on starting your own business while you are in college. You will develop skills to build on, and you will make much more than just an hourly rate. Start with your own interests, skills, and passions. If you have not identified them yet, think about what you like to do in your free time, what you notice when you shop, what you read for pleasure, where you like to spend time or browse, whom you admire, and what groups you would like to join. Survey what is needed and what is possible. Let your imagination wander anywhere, from catering and delivering food to students, to investing in the stock market, to creating a new network.

SERVICE LEARNING

The best part of the 1960s has returned in a new format. Altruism is back where it belongs—in college. On campuses everywhere, from Penn to Vanderbilt to Alverno, students are feeling the impulse to participate in and improve society by rolling up their sleeves to help communities in need. Service learning falls between volunteering with no obligations and interning in an organization. Service learning lets you earn academic credit for providing a semester's assistance to a community organization. You have to register for service learning classes or sign up for special projects, and you are usually required to write about the valuable insights or lessons you have learned in a journal or term paper. In your writing, you can include your personal reflections on the experience of performing service work right in the middle of the community at its neediest.

Are you interested in helping low-income earners figure out their taxes? Determining which services actually reach the neediest cases?

Helping juveniles to bypass hassles in court and get on with the process of rebuilding their lives? Projects like these exist if your professors and counselors are willing to design and facilitate them, to connect you with agencies, and to help you evaluate your findings. Besides getting credit, you'll learn lots about the relationship between the need and appropriate assistance. You will be taking the time to investigate how our society works from the inside out by combining academic theory with its real world application. Who will benefit? You, most of all, whether you are majoring in the social sciences, computer science, engineering, accounting, the humanities, or any other academic pursuit.

> *What are you doing for others?*
> —*Martin Luther King, Jr.*

VOLUNTEERING

Volunteering is the conscience of America. The Pew Research Center, which lists good deeds being done daily, has found that a substantial number of people in the United States volunteer their time to help shape their nation.

Beyond just doing good deeds, volunteers are willing to take action to build and rebuild the communities in which they want to live, whether through the schools, libraries, parks, museums, religious groups, hospitals, food banks, and city government or by just talking to kids in trouble. What you accomplish is greater than just giving aid to someone in need. Volunteering increases your sense of belonging and your community spirit.

You can sign up for one-day events, spend weekends rebuilding houses, or create a program around your own schedule. Los Angeles, for example, has over 40,000 nonprofit organizations eager to include you, no matter how skilled or unskilled you are. Some city and county agencies will cover your transportation and parking costs, even a meal, in return for your time.

Few volunteer programs have galvanized a nation's soul as much as President Kennedy's internationally focused Peace Corps, active since the 1960s. It is often rated as a peak experience in the lives of those who volunteered, studied another language, traveled to third-world countries, learned from the people they went to teach, and befriended and sometimes married other volunteers. President Jimmy Carter launched Habitat for Humanity, a program in which thousands of students are involved in every aspect of building homes for the poor. These volunteers are also building their own character in the process.

President Clinton's AmeriCorps, aimed at ending illiteracy within the United States, has invited volunteers to teach reading in elementary schools. Organized volunteer groups, such as VISTA and Teach for America, exist on nearly every college campus. Their purpose is to open a world and to share information, particularly for new immigrants who don't have the language skills to access it.

Believe it or not, volunteering turns out to be a great bargain. You will learn about others, but mostly, you learn more about yourself. You will gain confidence by discovering that you can be part of something greater than yourself and make a difference. You will also have a great time making friends with other volunteers whom you'd otherwise not meet. These benefits can be yours whether you're working on a political campaign or at an animal sanctuary. Finally, you might find inspiration from one activity that will grow into an internship, a service learning project, or even a career.

STRATEGIES FOR CONNECTING WITH THE REAL WORLD

There is a whole world of jobs and opportunities available for college students: working on campus internships, part-time and full-time jobs, work-study jobs, service learning, and volunteering. You can locate all these at your career center, volunteer center, or student activities center. There are printed lists and computer directories in your career center and online. You can connect directly to some of the sponsor organizations, from public to private to nonprofit, on your own through computer links.

It takes your willingness to be there, to make yourself indispensable, and to be part of the team to find work that will change your life. But you have to pay attention to the work, the people, and your own responses. Start now.

Chapter 7
Discovering Your Purpose

When we find our mission in life, we will enjoy our work.
—Richard N. Bolles

HOW TO KNOW WHAT YOU WANT TO DO

What are you going to do with your life after graduation? You will hear that question from everyone—your parents, your friends, your professors. You will ask yourself the same question repeatedly. If you know the answer, you are lucky. If you do not, join the secret conspiracy—uncertainty, like misery, loves company, and you have a lot of company.

If you have many interests, you will have many options. You cannot know for sure what the best path is before you choose. Uncertainty is a phenomenon that will accompany you most of your life. While no one predicted it, the current nature of the workplace and our own wish to continue developing have created a scenario in which most of us will change jobs, even careers, many times, perhaps more than six times in our working lives. While that may make a person sound unstable, it is the rate determined by the Department of Labor for changing technologies and economies as well as personal development. You will no doubt experience such rapid change yourself. You may even be more fulfilled because of it. But change within successful careering is not like changing majors every semester. In fact, careers are not very much at all like college, where there are structured course requirements and benevolent professors. Successful careering requires your courage to explore, take risks, evaluate how you are doing, expand your horizons, and find what else you might do or be.

Here are some steps to match your skills and your passions to the marketplace. Start inside, by tapping your inner resources and finding your hidden and not-so-hidden talents, before you look outside at the world at large. Each of us longs to find our calling, a passionate pursuit that is congruent with our heart's desire. While you may already know or at least have an inkling of what your calling is, you may have to do detective work to find valuable clues in your life. It is worth the time to look back into your childhood to identify your own preferences, delights, and interests. Go as far back as you can remember. When you were a kid, did you collect stamps, sell lemonade or skateboards, produce the neighborhood variety show, organize a charity drive for school or church, build model houses in your basement, or write short stories or plays?

Take the time to write down these activities and what you recall about each. Then describe the part of the activity you cared about most. It might have been creating something new or finding something hidden, working solo or together with a group. Does it still hold true now? What you enjoyed so much then might still be intriguing to you now and critical to your future choice. If you were a collector, there is a good chance that you prefer being the complete master of a small but total body of knowledge. If so, you might now gear up for being an expert in a particular specialty. If you built models or painted T-shirts, perhaps at heart you are an artisan or artist. If you organized a fundraising drive or produced a play, you have the leadership skills to be a manager, producer, or entrepreneur. Even if nothing definite shows up, know that you are beginning to identify the dots of interest on your life map. Connecting those dots is the search for your profession.

In the same way, look over your past cocurricular activities in high school and college. I have seen a critical difference in the way students pick a major versus the way they choose activities. Your major might be a determination of the wishes of your parents or friends or whatever is considered "in" at the time. But your heartfelt interests are often more apparent in the clubs you select. What careers can you choose directly from your activities? To find out, list your activities and see what patterns emerge.

Through participating in activities, you will learn to develop skills and identify your natural talents. Each event in which you have participated has its skill-building rewards that carry over into real life, whether you go into planning, designing, budgeting, advertising, selling, science, publicity, or management.

Use the large network of your college alumni association. Try not to feel overwhelmed by the endless lists; make yourself read them over. They're available on your college Web site or in your alumni office. Then concentrate on the fields you would like to consider. Contact members and introduce yourself as a student of their alma mater. Ask for a ten-minute informational interview. I know that you will be astonished at their positive responses! Prepare questions to ask about their work, how they got started, what they originally wanted (if they knew), what surprises they found, and what they would have done differently. Don't forget to ask what advice they would give you just starting out. Take the initiative to describe your interests in college, your projects, papers, and activities, and even your work. In other words, take the risk of revealing yourself to them and hope that they like what you say. They might even hire you or refer you to a friend who can. Thank them for their time and interest in a note or e-mail with your permanent addresses, and be sure to keep their numbers so you can report your progress or ask for more leads later.

You may well be able to weave your core interests into a career. If you are an environmental studies major, don't wait passively for a good job to be listed. Instead, expand your chances by asking to work for your city council, a research group, a political party, the Sierra Club, or a sporting goods or wilderness store. While you are framing your diploma, do not be afraid to ask for any job, no matter how menial it may sound to you. Accept any offer, even to be a gofer, stock clerk, receptionist, or mail-room or delivery person. The point is to get in; once you learn the ropes and show that you are effective, you can climb higher.

For example, if your major is communications and you have been involved in student activities, you might find that you enjoy politics, events planning, producing, or managing associations and talent. Trust your interests and learn to build on them. Your professors, dean, and career counselor may be able to find you work as a paid assistant at your own or another college, a corporation, or a convention center. Also talk to the agents who represent the artists and speakers your university booked, even if you never thought of managing or agenting as a career. Managers and agents typically have liberal arts undergraduate degrees, were active in college life, and love selling "talent" to colleges. As a perk, they get to know celebrities. Agents, paid on commission, thrive on selling and dealing well with people on both sides of the table. The same holds true for executive directors of associations and foundations. You may never have heard of these careers. And you may not know what you will eventually do, but just starting in the field will help point the way. You are likely to need at least a master's degree later, but you can try out an interesting job before you make your decision about graduate school.

The original meaning of *career* is *to progress through life*. The original meaning of *success* is *one thing after another*, like the succession of presidents. What is the difference between *career* and *success?* None! They actually mean the same thing! Both imply movement and growth, rather than a fixed point or position. These definitions of such familiar words are loaded with weight and provide fresh insight about the inevitable choices we face, not only at graduation, but throughout our lives. We will always need information, insight, and motivation to debunk the myths that lead to distorted expectations.

MYTHS THAT LEAD TO UNREALISTIC EXPECTATIONS

Here are some of the most common misconceptions that can interfere with finding your true direction.

Myth: Success Means Finding the Right Career

Remember, the Department of Labor's statistics predict that most of us will move through many different careers, possibly six or more, and move within each of them to as many as fifteen different jobs. While this is not at all what our grandparents or parents did, it is common now. In the traditional employment model, workers traded lifetime loyalty to a company to get job security. The new mobility, like it or not, demands taking total responsibility for managing your own career and your own money. Self-management is more necessary than ever; it is precisely what this book is about.

Even so, you don't have to prepare for your first job or career without help; far from it. Learn to use the services and counselors in your career center. Get help or coaching to meet your immediate goals of finding an internship or landing your first job after graduation. Asking for advice must become a regular practice in order to achieve success throughout your life. The strategy is to build your confidence by constantly developing your skills and by connecting with people so you can be ready for opportunities when they come along. Make it a lifelong habit to get the help and leads you need from the most appropriate sources, and you will learn to return the favor with thanks and help in kind.

What if you don't have a strong specific interest? When you need a real career direction, not knowing feels like a curse. Your versatility improves your odds greatly. You probably are not aware that all corporations employ a wide range of workers, from engineering, research, and design, to sales and marketing, accounting and data management, human resources, and customer and legal services. They also need chefs, gardeners, art specialists, insurance agents, and investors. Additionally, corporations hire consultants who have their own staff. Companies attend trade shows, which, in turn, have their own services. Look online to see the range of top local companies, or those in cities in which you would like to live. If you start somewhere—anywhere—you will learn about these organizations and meet people who will turn you on to more possibilities.

You are not finished choosing when you pick a major; you are only just beginning. Even though it is baffling and overwhelming at times, having the luxury to make a choice is your inheritance.

Myth: Self-Reliance Should Be Total

Reading biographies of prominent people can be a great educator and motivator. You will find that most accomplished people have not only taken more risks and engaged in more negotiations than less successful people, but they surprisingly have relied on more resources and used more connections. The difference is between appropriate self-reliance (which is good) and total self-reliance (which is bad or even impossible). Learn to give up that false god of complete independence. While it is true that you have to initiate your contracts and carry through on what you have promised to do, do not be fooled into thinking you have to do it all by yourself. Do you know the expression to "pull yourself up by your bootstraps?" That's an impossibility, unless the boots are nailed to the ceiling! I hope that while you are in college you can debunk the bootstrap myth and develop networks and strategies to link you to relationships and collaborations.

Myth: If You Don't Know What You Want to Do, There's Something Wrong

More than just an institution from which you can get a degree, college is the place where you can actually shape your dreams and yourself. Who you are and what you want to be can be either a definite concept within you or a dormant seed. For most people, discovering their talents and finding suitable work takes a long time. Identifying dreams is a continuing process, because people grow and change just as the marketplace does. The skills you need to cultivate a fantasy and shape it into reality must continue to be honed.

Ask yourself what your dream might be. Is it really yours or is it your family's choice? Does it fill you up or drain you? All the proposed activities in the preceding chapters—actively developing mentor relationships, participating in clubs and activities, participating in internships and part-time work, using papers and projects for investigation—are strategies to connect you to worlds of interest outside in order to find what mirrors your own world or inspires you. Through such active engagement in college, you will begin to discover your identity through your interests and skills and passions. You have the fire within to pursue your calling, the core of your authentic work. Your work in college and ever after is to find that fire and to keep it burning. Your goal is to discover your work and then give yourself over to that process.

Most students are not sure what careers to choose, even those who have chosen professional careers. When that happens, then they feel awkward, even ashamed, of not knowing, as if something were wrong with them. I wish I could erase that awful and debilitating feeling from those who have it.

It is completely appropriate not to be certain when there is so much to choose from and when you are so capable of doing so many different things. You make better choices only when you have experience through internships and/or part-time jobs, as well as the guidance of career counselors and professors. It would take more than a lifetime to learn everything about the world of work; obviously, you cannot do that. Start with your best subjects and find work that leads from that. Once you start with a company, an organization, or a profession, you will develop more knowledge of what beckons you.

There is a perception of status about a hierarchy of professions. But if those "top" careers are not interesting to you or your ability does not lie within them, allow yourself to experiment in other fields to find what is interesting. You may find your calling or find that you are ready to choose. What other people want for you might work out, but you are the one who will have to do the job day after day, week after week, and year after year. Becoming truer to yourself is more fulfilling than pleasing others.

When you choose a career only to satisfy your craving for status, you can lose yourself. The only way to test this is to work at the jobs *you* want versus those that *they* (friends or family) want for you. Interview those whom you admire as well as the high-status personalities. Find your own answer. It might surprise you. One humanities major went to medical school at his parents' insistence. He hated the ordeal of the four-year program and the intense internship that followed, but he couldn't drop out or switch. Instead, he found, through his residency and training, that psychiatry was closely linked to his love of literature. Once he could narrow the field of medicine to suit himself, he led a fulfilling life. In contrast, another medical student graduated, interned, and took a residency in dermatology. When her practice became too demanding a business, it grew unfulfilling. She gave it up and joined a pharmaceutical firm as a researcher, her truer calling.

In pursuing another professional career, law, I have found that some lawyers do not end up practicing law at all. Many become professors, managers, entrepreneurs, journalists or politicians. Their training is not wasted; it provides access to thoughts, ideas, and connections to life that would be hard to find otherwise. Similarly, some psychologists find that their clinical practice is too limiting and therefore pursue leadership-oriented positions, such as marketing, management, or journalism, making full use of their keen understanding of people.

Myth: Males and Females Should Have Different Careers

Because women and men are so different, should they should go after different careers? All research about gender proves otherwise. While the generalized behavioral tasks that separate males from females have held in the past, individual talents and preferences prevail today.

Men are expected to be leaders in business, sports, and the professions and often achieve just that. But they can also make fine nurses as well as doctors; team members as well as managers; counselors or therapists as well as athletes or salesmen; and teachers as well as soldiers.

Women are frequently expected to be caregivers, but they can also make excellent college and corporate presidents as well as teachers; salespeople, scientists and analysts as well as technicians; and customer service representatives as well as artists.

Brain research is showing that, while men and women have similar IQs, they often are acculturated to think and act in different ways. Women manage more by consensus, a trait that is increasingly valued, and are better at helping a group to collaborate and cooperate. Men, less socially conscious in their job behavior, are often more risk-oriented, which is also valued. It becomes obvious that men and women can learn to develop both traits and be rewarded for them. Successful men and women tell me that they don't think of themselves as any gender while they are doing their best work—they are simply "doers."

Yet the major difference between the genders is self-confidence, and that may be key to our expectations. Men are often more self-confident and believe that they can do the job even if they have not done it before. Most corporations that hire young men expect that they will thrive and be promoted. In fact, for a man not to be perceived as doing well, he has to perform quite badly. These same corporate managers do not expect as much from young women; yet women must prove their worth even to stay at a constant level.

Studies of United States Presidents—all male so far—reveal a deeper side of performance having to do with expectations. A significant number of our presidents were their mother's favorites. They also all come from families in which the mothers were the most ambitious coaches and dominant forces for their sons. Their mothers' expectations became a self-fulfilling prophecy. So does the extreme opposite. Studies of poor and failing young men and women reveal that there was little or no support for their studies and work. If support and expectation are the keys to success, then both men and women can achieve far greater things with them than without them.

When I coach professionals who come to me with dilemmas, whether it's finding the right work or dealing with a difficult boss or situation, I cannot help but notice this difference in self-confidence. Men, no matter what their education or work history, present their best side to me before they reveal their problems. I have to ask many questions to find where they are faltering or where they might be better suited. Women, on the other hand, often present their most vulnerable side to me first. I cannot tell what they have accomplished until I ask. My first task with women is to help raise their confidence and self-awareness.

My goal for everyone is to find the core of their talents and yearnings and help resolve their dilemmas so that they improve, contribute more, become more recognized, or else change to something more satisfying. It is difficult to do that alone without support.

Myth: Your Career Must Derive Directly from Your Major

Many majors drive careers, such as in the engineering and accounting professions. But if your major does not lead you toward something that you want to pursue, perhaps your activities will. Here is an example of someone who created a successful career out of her activities, outshining her major. In a wonderful conversation with Abigail Phillips, the original "Dear Abby," I learned how this popular syndicated columnist actually crafted her career. In college, she had to prove to her parents through daily letters that she was going to class and doing her homework. Her favorite college activity was going to fraternity parties. I asked what she was interested in—the boys, the dancing? "Gossip," she answered. And gossip fueled her writing for the campus paper's first column on that subject. As "Dear Abby," her writing had elements of both parable and gossip, which she combined to create great, enduring, and entertaining advice for readers for decades.

Take a different look at your own interests. If you, like "Dear Abby," are fixated on going to parties, ask yourself how parties can lead you to a satisfying career. Start exploring the following fields to see what calls to you:

- Catering for parties, corporate events, weddings, or fund raisers
- Designing or selling costumes
- Designing sets for TV, movies, school productions, and local theater
- Managing campaigns, from local offices to national parties
- Lobbying on a state or national basis for a cause or a special interest
- Agenting for actors and writers
- Brokering for a business
- Planning meetings for professional associations, corporations, hotels, and convention centers
- Agenting for speakers for universities and professional organizations
- Performing product placement duties for movie and TV productions and commercials
- Scouting locations for movie/TV/commercial shoots or corporate affairs
  - Marketing, manufacturing, or selling party favors

You won't skid if you stay in a rut!
—Kin Hubbard

USING THE CAREER CENTER

Most students state that their main purpose for going to college is to get a better job. But many report that after they graduate, they are disappointed with the work they find. They admit that they did not use the college's career center before the last month of their last semester, if ever. Your college has a career center that is offered free to you. The center's counselors can guide you in the process of discovering your best skills, but only if you visit and take advantage of their services. It is the first best career step to take. When you visit your career center, you can schedule time for individual career counseling with caring, dedicated professionals who will guide you to make the best choices and can act as your coaches while you are enrolled.

Each career center is staffed with a group of professional career counselors whose sole mission is to help you find your best career. Career counselors have had graduate training in assessing career choices. They can also administer vocational and personality tests to help interpret your scores. They can share contacts in the business, arts, and service communities both on and off campus. They can help determine whether your major is working for you and how to commit to it or to change it. They can offer insights leading you to a variety of sources of career information. They will listen to your experience and steer you toward appropriate leads. They can provide you with information such as books, videotapes, databases, resources for ideas and leads, and organizations to contact so that you can understand where that major might lead. They can direct you to ways to get experience and more mentoring. They can also motivate you to engage more fully with your professors, your coursework, and student activities in order to discover your interests and talents.

They can assist you in writing your résumé and cover letter, coach you to present yourself to recruiters and other interviewers, guide you in making a choice, and even help negotiate the best starting offer possible. They can be great sources of support and powerful allies—but only if you ask them. Career counselors need to be cultivated. Take the initiative and make an appointment. Get to know them and let them know about you.

Your career center presents workshops on a range of topics, from how to choose a career to how to conduct a job search, along with hands-on training for the process. They produce job fairs and encourage you to meet prospective employers so that you will make critical connections. They also arrange career conferences and events, hoping you will attend in order to learn about career paths and experiences, as well as to hear advice from successful people in fields you want to enter, even those that you may not have considered yet. They help you make connections with and compare employers so that you can make better choices. Plus, they provide on-campus interviewing schedules so that you can meet with employers and compare recruiters in order to get the best possible offer. They also coach you so that you interview competitively.

Career counselors might encourage you to test out your major and get on-the-job experience by signing up for an internship or two. They will help you find a part-time job that will give you a better overview of an industry or a company as well as leads and access. They have job listings for part-time jobs, both on and off campus, to suit your goals.

They might even persuade you to take your junior semester or year abroad and expand your world and work view. They help you look ahead and provide information and advice on selecting a graduate school, either for immediate application or for a year or two following graduation.

Facts of Life in Majors and Careers

1. *If you want to be an engineer, lawyer, doctor, nurse, technician, biologist, psychologist, or career counselor, you must select majors and graduate degrees. Often these practitioners are required to be certified, licensed, or otherwise eligible.*

2. *Many other professions and careers do not require a specific major or degree. College presidents, politicians, entrepreneurs, producers, managers, inventors, researchers, and sales and marketing people come from every kind of major, degree, and personality type.*

3. *Your first job is not your only career. But you will learn how to begin working toward it.*

A tip: Use your college's career center early, even in your freshman year. *Do not wait* until the final month before graduation to make your first appointment. Counseling centers regularly offer private sessions and workshops in all aspects of career planning, from choosing a career and determining what you can do with your major, to selecting an internship and getting a job. Use the center well and often. Do not shortchange yourself by graduating without its help.

Run—don't walk—to your career center, whether or not you are ready to graduate. Get career information and advice before you have to make a career decision. If you do not have a clue about what to choose, get tested and see if the results match your own criteria. Sign up for workshops about job searching and job interviewing strategies. Don't just sit there: be *active*. Participate. Turn your college experiences into a kind of personal laboratory, a process very much like developing photographs in a darkroom, where the image gradually emerges from blank paper in a tray of chemicals. The chemistry in your life can be your career counselor, your professors, your internship supervisor, an idea that hits you out of the blue, or an inspiration that comes when you are reading or doing something else.

All serious daring starts from within. —*Eudora Welty*	**GET TO KNOW THYSELF** Knowing yourself and being able to describe yourself to other people are critical abilities in themselves. Here are some questions that

you can ask yourself to guide you in the process. Think of the exercise as a way of brainstorming with yourself to realize who you have been, what you have enjoyed, and what you hope for. It is worth the effort to achieve self-reflection; not working to divine some of your own answers means that you will always elude yourself. Of course, we do hope that others will see us better than we can see ourselves and explain our talents to us. However, having an initial self-evaluation steps up the process before you ask anyone else or before you go to the career center. Try working with the "Interview Yourself" exercise at the end of this chapter. Take the results to the career center to help you and your counselor aim more accurately. If you would like to build on your own answers, there are assessments you can take also. Why not? We are used to tests that rank us, so why not a test to reveal our personalities and interests? Why not a test to match our hidden desires to an appropriate pursuit?

Personality Assessments

A personality assessment can offer an astonishingly accurate snapshot of you. Yes, most of us love to take such a test to learn more about ourselves. Strangely enough, we get little feedback about who we are, what our personalities are, and how they compare to and with others. Learning about our own style of behavior and basic personality characteristics is more than just interesting; it is informative, motivating, and often comforting. The Myers-Briggs Type Inventory (MBTI), Keirsey Temperament Sorter, or Kolbe Index, for example, are easy-to take, multiple-choice, self-reporting assessments that can yield amazing insights. However, understand that your answers aren't set in stone; if you take this assessment over time, your answers will likely change as you do.

One of the side benefits to taking a personality test is to discover that we all have different ways of behaving. Finding out that most people don't behave exactly like you do is illuminating. Not only that; you get to see that there is no right behavioral style. Your test result will describe you in many situations. For example, while you may be impulsive or a quick starter, others make their decisions only after careful analysis. If you are more interested in how something operates, you will realize that many others do not care at all about the process. If you are independent and want to do your own thing in your own time, you might be surprised to see that many more people, who feel a lot more comfortable with structure, are happier working hard for a larger organization with more defined roles.

When it comes to personalities and careers, people have all sorts of options, not one defined "right" choice. The key to job satisfaction is to understand your strengths and weaknesses, likes and dislikes, so you can make choices that are appropriate for you. Because most people work with other people, it helps to understand how the people around you can affect your job performance and possibilities.

Vocational Assessments

In addition to personality tests, there are various vocational assessments that might give you some clue about what you're like and what you might like to do. Every career center does, indeed, provide personality and vocational testing for a vast number of students who simply do not yet know what they want to do. Many of these tests, available online with immediate scoring, can be interpreted by your career counselor. There are a variety of interactive computerized career assessments, such as SIGI Plus, FOCUS, the Strong, the Holland typology of nearly 300 occupations, among others. These career assessments have a number of benefits:

- They try to correlate your likes and dislikes, interests, and values with a databank of thousands of responses by other individuals already in designated occupations.
- They may help you to articulate your priorities and values.
- They provide a starting point of discussion for your career counseling sessions.
  - They provide a sketch of your personality and behavioral preferences compared to others.

However, these assessments are far from foolproof; don't rely on their accuracy to reveal who you really are or what you should do. Because they tend to categorize skills, interests, and personality types in a general way for a specific time in space, vocational assessments can point to your preferences expressed at the time of the test. They cannot, alas, perfectly predict your career, nor can they consider future changes in your interests or skills any more than they can predict the marketplace's future. They are limited to matching your interests to those of other people who took the test and whose later career success was known. Yet, when you think of it, each and every profession contains a multitude of types of work and ways to do it. That rich variety, in turn, attracts and promotes many different personalities, styles, and motivations.

Consider the law profession as an example. Even though the law school curriculum and bar association tests are standardized, every aspect of the legal profession demands a different personality. Trial lawyers are more dramatic, aggressive, and spontaneous. Typically, patent lawyers are more introverted and detail-oriented. Family law attorneys are more psychologically attuned to individual clients. Estate lawyers are more financially adept. Corporate attorneys tend to be more business-oriented. Entertainment lawyers, liking celebrity, often become celebrities themselves. Law professors, having been among the highest ranked in their law classes, remain the most theoretical. Can you tell which personality is best suited for a lawyer? Right—there is no one answer!

Add new jobs to the mix. In every decade, one-third of all careers are newly created. That's not just a hunch, but it is statistically accurate according to the Department of Labor. Vocational tests, based on history rather than prediction, obviously cannot include career paths that have not emerged yet. Vocational assessments constantly need to be updated to include newly created careers.

Finally, there is you. You change and so does your score, even from morning to afternoon, and certainly from year to year. However, despite their limitations, vocational tests can be a great start to recognizing the glimmerings of your inner self. Think of them as the sieve in a process much like panning for gold. You are not the only one who does not know what to be or do. Most people do not know what we want and even have a hard time recognizing it when they see it. As a former labor negotiator, I remember that the most difficult problem of all was getting people to realize what they *really* want, not what they think they want or what they think others expect from them. "Finding yourself"—an odd expression that conveys the feeling of being lost—is a learning process that comes from activities, evaluation, and experimentation.

Sometimes it is a mistake to categorize yourself. Say you are interested in being both a writer and a public speaker. If you took a personality test that measures introversion versus extroversion, where do you think you would place? How can you be both, when you write alone yet speak before people? Most likely, you are not only one type of personality all of the time. You may enjoy the solo pleasure of writing but also relish the time when you present your message to an audience. You may excel and be comfortable in both arenas.

The same dichotomy exists for professors who spend many solitary hours doing research and then present lectures with their data. Finding the most comfortable balance between being with many people and being alone is important. Why? By discovering yourself, you will know where you feel most alive and when you feel most drained. An appropriate career choice leads you to identify where you feel most alive. Sometimes that choice comes early in your life; sometimes it can come only later, with experience.

Identifying Your Skills

Here is a list of the most common skills that are used by people who work. You will, no doubt, see many that you possess and can discuss and many that you might be interested in but have not yet experienced. Check all the skills that you already have. Put two checks beside those you would like to continue to use. Star the skills you would like to try. Remember, there is no right answer. Every skill is necessary to some type of work.

- Reading
- Writing
- Discussing
- Listening
- Creating
- Generating ideas
- Reporting information
- Analyzing information
- Thinking logically
- Thinking independently
- Applying technical knowledge
- Testing machines or people
- Inventing
- Repairing or operating machines
- Editing and correcting
- Troubleshooting
- Explaining and teaching
- Speaking in public
- Coordinating projects or conferences
- Helping others
- Motivating and encouraging
- Managing groups or projects
- Leading
- Being a strong team member
- Following through
- Working behind the scenes
- Planning
- Scheduling and evaluating
- Budgeting
- Building trust
- Interacting with people on projects as team member and then leader
- Socializing or networking

Interviewing Yourself

Your entry into real life begins with an exploration of yourself. You are more than the sum of your height, weight, age, race, socioeconomic level, grades, and/or work history. You are also your ideas, aspirations, likes and dislikes, fears, interests, abilities, predilections, beliefs, and dreams. But you are often blind to these aspects in yourself.

Try answering the following questions before you visit your career center. The more you can tell your career counselors about yourself and what you want to find out, the better they can help.

1. Identify your thoughts about yourself.
2. Categorize what you have done.
3. Inventory the things you like.
4. Discuss your philosophy or how you approach life.
5. Identify what kind of help and information you would like.

Questions for Self-Evaluation

These kernel sentences, in which you complete the beginning statements, are designed to help you move toward your interests and strengths. Some of your responses may surprise you! Answer them on separate sheets and keep the sheets with the book. Your answers will be very valuable in conferences with your counselor or professors.

1. My academic focus is on the following fields or subjects:
2. At present, my career objective is:
3. What I think I do best is:
4. What I do just to please myself is:
5. I would like to improve:
6. My real talents and skills, of which people are not aware, are:
7. People usually count on me for:
8. What I regard as most rewarding about a job or activity is (rate them 1–5, 5 being the most rewarding):
    a. Awards won
    b. Satisfaction
    c. Fame or recognition
    d. Creating solo
    e. Money
    f. Excitement
    g. Praise from peers
    h. Feeling of involvement

9. The music I like best is:
10. I pay attention to news about:
11. Sports I follow are:
12. Ideas that grab my interest are about:
13. People I care about are involved in:
14. When my spirits or energy are low, then I take time to:
15. The things I would most like to learn more about are:
16. My strong points are:
17. My weak points are:
18. The activities I have loved doing the most over my lifetime:
19. The activities I loved when I was between 5 and 9 years old:
20. The activities I loved when I was between 10 and 14 years old:
21. The activities I loved when I was between 15 and 18 years old:
22. If I could pick a career based on any one of the activities listed in questions 18–21, it would be:
23. My family thinks I should be:
24. Others who know me believe I am all about:
25. The people whom I do things for would describe me and my work as:
26. The things I would most like to learn more about are:
27. For my next birthday, I would like my friends to:
29. Other good qualities I possess are:
30. If income and responsibilities were not factors, I would like to:
31. If I could do whatever I wanted for a day, I would:
32. If I could do whatever I wanted for a month, I would:
33. If I could do whatever I wanted for two years, I would:
34. The story, fable, or anecdote most relevant to my life is:
35. If I could, I would like to be known for:
36. My heroes and role models are:
37. The people I admire most are:
38. The current people I admire most (and why) are:
39. The historical people I admire most are:
40. The careers I most admire are:
41. The obstacles my heroes overcame are:
42. The talents, skills, or values I admire or share with my heroes are:
43. What motivated my heroes in their life's work:
44. What lesson from my heroes' lives could I apply to my career:
45. The best I can hope for my career might be something like:

For the next three questions, again use separate sheets and keep them in this book. Use them when consulting with professors or career advisors. I've divided working life into three periods: now, next, and later. For each of those periods, describe your desires in the areas listed. If you can't answer a question, make your best estimate.

46. Now
    a. Position:
    b. Kind of organizations:
    c. Type of assignment:
    d. How long you might spend with each:
    e. What changes might happen and how:
    f. What important things you would do besides work:
    g. What you would do when you do not have to work:

47. Next
    a. Position:
    b. Kind of organizations:
    c. Type of assignment:
    d. How long you might spend with each:
    e. What changes might happen and how:
    f. What important things you would do besides work:
    g. What you would do when you do not have to work:

48. Later
    a. Position:
    b. Kind of organizations:
    c. Type of assignment:
    d. How long you might spend with each:
    e. What changes might happen and how:
    f. What important things you would do besides work:
    g. What you would do when you do not have to work:

49. If, in the future, you were *Time* magazine's "Person of the Year," what would you like to be known for? Write that cover essay now. It may be the most illuminating report you will ever write.

Chapter 8
Finding Your First Job

Love is work made visible.

—*Kahlil Gibran*

THE SEARCH PROCESS

Finding a Right Career

If you are graduating soon, think of this transition period like your old growing pains—a temporary discomfort you have to endure for the sake of your fervently wished-for results: a job! But no matter how sophisticated your academic program has been, you are in for a huge adjustment in this transition from college to your first full-time job. You do not have to do this by yourself, however. Your college career center has career counselors, programs, and services designed specifically to help you manage a career choice, as well as the job search process.

Finding the right job or career is still the #1 concern of 83% of college students.
— The Student Monitor

Ways to Find Jobs

Do not overlook these steps to finding a great job:

1. Network by finding and using all the leads from your career counselors, professors, family, friends, and people

whom you have met through clubs, lectures, internships, part-time jobs, and job fairs.

2. Log onto job listings and links from your college career center's Web site.

3. Check for leads from the bulletin boards that line the hallways and offices of the department where your major is located.

4. Use your career center's library to research companies and other institutions from databases, brochures, handouts, and books.

5. Attend the job fairs held on campus, as well as in your city.

6. Sign up for on-campus interviews for practice if you are not sure that you are interested.

7. Don't be upset if there are too many choices; choosing is always a difficult process.

8. Ask yourself this question: If you knew you would not fail, what would you do? Trust yourself and go for it!

The Job Search Process

After you have selected a few organizations or fields, it pays off to organize the job search process, as well as you can. Yes, it will take planning and time. It is called a "process" for a reason. If you do not do excellent and precise work on your résumé, cover letter, and letters of recommendation, then you probably will not even get an interview.

Here's an overview of the entire job search process (with full explanations following) that you'll be going through:

1. Prepare a focused and clear résumé to suit each job for which you are applying.

2. List five references from your professors, coaches, sponsors, and employers. At the end of your résumé, state that references are available. Include the list on a separate sheet labeled References.

3. Get five letters of recommendation from professors and employers.

4. Learn all you can about the many kinds of organizations and the wide variety of jobs within them from your career counselor, professors, internships, research papers, the Web, and from libraries or bookstores.

5. Research the organization before you interview with them. Demonstrate that you are familiar with them and can meet their requirements.

6. Write a cover letter to explain why you are applying for the job.
7. Demonstrate that you know and can meet the requirements for the job through classwork and real work experience from internships, part-time jobs, volunteer work, and/or a fellowship on or off campus.
8. Learn about the structure and art of interviewing through workshops and practice with career counselors to improve your self-presentation.
9. Convince the employer of what you can do for the company, rather than ask what it can do for you. Get coaching from your career counselors about best and appropriate questions and answers.
10. Practice interviewing through your career center's on-campus program to polish your presentation skills.
11. If there are no jobs available at the first job on top of your list, consider the number two job for a trial year, learning as much as you can.
12. Go to conferences; follow up with ideas and people, including attendees and speakers, as well as the placement room where jobs are posted.
13. Take the risk of linking with others, finding shared interests and values to talk about. This life skill will do more than just help you get the job: it will put more enjoyment into it.

You are going to be in charge of your career and will be solely responsible for yourself. You will get to shape your life from now on; no one else will. But for sure, you will keep returning to the job search process throughout your career. There's no shortcut for the anxiety it brings. If you can, think of it as a treasure hunt; you just might strike gold.

RÉSUMÉ SMARTS

What You Really Need to Know About Résumés

A résumé is a document stating that you exist as a real person who has gone to college and experienced some kind of responsibility. Think of the résumé as a qualifier that allows you entry to any job search. You have to have a résumé, but it cannot get you the job by itself. No one can look only at you or what appears on your résumé to determine how capable you are. It is up to you to tell them in person. That means you have to get past being embarrassed or feeling shy, or even fraudulent. But do not lie on your résumé. Do not claim that you have either experiences or degrees that you have not earned.

Your résumé has to look professional. In other words, it has to look like most of the résumés of those people who are already in the workplace. For guides, look at sample résumés for the industries you are interested in; there are dozens of résumé guidebooks in the career center, libraries, bookstores, and online. Use good sense, too. Submit your one-page résumé on white paper and/or online with no more than two fonts and one type of bullet. You have to express yourself in a particular format in appropriate, clear English—a harder task than you might think. Ask a counselor or friend to edit and proofread it for you.

List and group your recent accomplishments in categories such as "Education" and "Work Experience." Specify what you have accomplished academically, including honors and awards, as well as your experience in cocurricular activities, internships, part- and full-time work, and volunteer events. Employers prefer a chronological résumé, working from the present back in time, so they can easily see when you had which experience.

The Most Desirable Résumé Form

The typical résumé is a direct account of yourself, telling where to contact you and why you are qualified. List your education and experience, going backwards from the present to the past, on one page. It must look professional and be accurate; typos are unacceptable.

Things to Include in Your Résumé

1. Heading: name, address, phone, fax, and e-mail. Include a permanent address, for example your parents' address if yours is temporary.
2. Job objective: write exactly the job description for which you are applying (which means that you may have many versions of your résumé to send out).
3. Education: your university, its location, your major, and your degree, including honors. Omit high school unless it is a prestigious prep school.
4. Work experience: both part- and full-time jobs including the organizations' names, job titles, dates worked, and a list of your responsibilities.
5. Cocurriculars: include activities and roles you played.

6. Languages: list foreign languages that you speak or read, if any.
7. Technical skills: mention computer programs and/or software languages in which you have proficiency (e.g., C++, Perl, Fortran, JavaScript, SQL).
8. References: list names of professionals willing to provide a reference for you on a separate page. Have several letters of recommendation ready.

Words of Caution

- Don't write a general job objective that reflects what you want from life, such as "a challenging position that will let me learn and increase my skills." Instead, make your objective fit the job you're applying for exactly. It should be brief and to the point, even if you are not sure what that entails. The recruiter wants to know what *you* will do for the company, not what it will do for you.
- Don't list your salary requirement, except when explicitly asked, and even then, only state a range of what is normal, after you find this out from your career counselor.
- You don't have to include your GPA unless it is impressive.
- You don't have to reveal any personal information, such as what you look like, your height, weight, race, religion, gender.
- Omit all jokes unless you're going for a comedy job in the entertainment industry.
- Don't be afraid of sounding too strong. This is not a time to be modest and hope some recruiter can read between the lines and see how smart you really are.
- Don't have any typos, misspellings, sloppy language, or smudge marks, which will almost certainly disqualify you.

Why Be so Careful?

Employers are looking for skills that you have begun to develop and can bring to the job. These skills are often acquired through a class and an activity, e.g., an English major who learns technical writing. They can be acquired through experience, e.g., the student government representative who develops strong motivation and consensus-building skills. Such skills, while closely related (and with some overlap), can be divided into subsets: working with people, things, and/or data/information.

The following are ways for you to demonstrate your career skills:

- List all the jobs you've ever held, including part-time, full-time, and summer jobs, as well as internships and volunteer work.
- List all classes taken, based on your transcript.
- Note those skills and experiences you have identified on your résumé, and keep the list for future reference.
- Write a verb phrase for each of the jobs and classes listed. Don't begin with "I" but only with strong, action verbs. Use the following list as a guide.

Your Goal

You want to write a résumé that will land you an interview. Show that you can actually perform the specific job for which you are applying. Read the job description and then demonstrate that you can perform the role by giving examples of your experiences in part-time jobs, full-time jobs, internships, volunteer activities, leadership in clubs and activities, and class projects. Mirror the same language used in the job description. Yes, you might have to write different résumés for different jobs. Be positive and demonstrate that you can do the job.

Can you really know how to do the job? Not unless you already held such a position. Everyone knows that you cannot do the job before you learn exactly what it is and how to do it. You learn the job only by doing it. That's the secret of life. Your résumé should include the responsibilities and leadership skills you've taken on or developed in clubs, internships, and jobs. Send your résumé and cover letter and then call within a week to ask for an appointment for an interview.

Employers tell me confidentially that even though they receive many e-mails and snail-mailed résumés, they hire only after a face-to-face meeting. So do not think that by just sending your résumés out, you can sit back and just wait for calls. Getting a job is not like turning in papers to your professors with the expectation of a grade. Your job search is just the beginning of your active driving force.

If you are graduating soon, compose your résumé, both on paper and on the online résumé matching services available at most college career centers. You need a password to log on to your center's computer so that you can enter your education and experience data.

Dumb Résumé Errors from Smart Students

- *Typographical, grammatical, or spelling errors.* These errors scream out carelessness, poor education and/or lack of intelligence. Have at

Verbs to Highlight Your Skills

accomplished	decreased	handled	participated	set up
achieved	delegated	headed	perceived	sold
activated	delivered	improved	performed	simplified
adjusted	designed	implemented	persuaded	strengthened
administered	detailed	improvised	planned	solved
analyzed	directed	increased	prepared	sorted
applied	demonstrated	influenced	presented	staffed
approved	distributed	initiated	presided	started
arranged	discovered	innovated	processed	streamlined
attained	devised	inspected	produced	stressed
attended	developed	inspired	programmed	stretched
brought	disapproved	installed	projected	structured
budgeted	earned	instituted	promoted	succeeded
built	edited	instructed	proved	supervised
changed	effected	interpreted	proposed	supported
clarified	encouraged	integrated	provided	taught
closed	engineered	introduced	purchased	traced
conceived	established	interviewed	recruited	tracked
completed	enlarged	investigated	related	traded
communicated	evaluated	invented	reduced	transferred
consolidated	estimated	launched	recommended	trained
conducted	examined	led	redesigned	traveled
constructed	expanded	made	reported	transformed
created	experienced	maintained	reshaped	trimmed
consolidated	expedited	managed	researched	uncovered
coordinated	facilitated	molded	reevaluated	united
customized	forecasted	monitored	reviewed	unified
converted	formulated	motivated	revised	updated
counseled	formed	negotiated	reorganized	wrote
controlled	founded	originated	scheduled	
contracted	generated	operated	selected	
dealt	governed	organized	served	
defined	guided	oversaw	serviced	

least two people proofread your résumé. Don't rely solely on your computer's spell-checker or grammar-checker.

- *Too hard to read.* A poorly typed or reproduced résumé is unprofessional. Use a standard typeface in the 12-point size. Asterisks, bullets, underlining, boldface, and italics should be used only to make the document easier to read, not fancier. Again, get a professional's opinion.

- *Too sparse.* Give more than the bare essentials, especially when describing related work experience, skills, accomplishments, activities, interests, and club memberships. They give employers important information. Including membership in a professional association is helpful to employers who wish to hire the most ambitious and focused people.

- *Irrelevant information.* You must customize each résumé for each position you seek. Of course, include all education and work experience, but emphasize only relevant experience, skills, accomplishments, activities, and hobbies. Do not include marital status, age, sex, children, height, weight, health, or religious affiliation.
- *Generic.* The employer needs to feel you are interested in that particular position with his or her particular company, so don't use a résumé sample without personalizing it.
- *Boring.* Make your résumé readable and dynamic. Use active verbs to describe what you have accomplished in past jobs. Take advantage of your vocabulary and avoid repeating words, especially the first word in a section. Begin every statement with an action verb.
- *Overly modest.* The résumé should emphasize your qualifications in competition with other applicants. Put your best foot forward.
- *Not knowing the employer.* Ignorance is not bliss. Your career center can help you find out what the prospective company does, what the position involves, and whether you will be a fit, before submitting your résumé. Research the company, how it is structured, the position, and about the type of employee the company typically hires. Find out about the company from its Web site, which includes information about its background, community involvement, special events, executive bios, and past annual reports as well as available jobs. Get the name of the department head and call. Explain that you are considering applying to the company, and ask for next steps, to whom to send your résumé, and thank that person for the information.
- *Not knowing the employees.* If possible, interview someone who does the same job. In addition to finding out the duties, ask if there is on-the-job training, and whether they value education over experience. Ask what the employees like about the position and the company; more important, ask what they don't like about it.

Your résumé, then, translates what you have done for yourself into what you will do at the next job. Your résumé won't get you a job by itself, but you can't get a job without it.

Everyone hates writing résumés. Some students take days to do it. Still, it's a version of you on one page. Be as professional and selective as you can. You're worth it.

FIRST CONTACT

Etiquette for E-mailing

- Assume everyone will read your e-mail. Do not write anything you would be embarrassed about. Do not be too casual. Write in full, professional sentences.
- Type in your formal name. Do not use a cute handle that will diminish you in the eyes of the employer (e.g., Katherine, not Kat).
- Type in the specific subject line: Application, Inquiry, or Thank you.
- Follow the online application format.
  1. Use a plain text format.
  2. Use the e-mail window to write your cover letter.
  3. Use caps in the words Education and Work Experience rather than underline or boldface, which tend to get lost in the body of the e-mail.
  4. Set a professional writing tone.
  5. Send the e-mail to yourself first to see what it looks like on screen.
  6. Use spell-check and grammar-check; then do a final human spell-check and grammar-check.
- Use a professional salutation; learn the correct names and titles of those to whom you are writing.
- Be brief. Outline your message first so you can organize your thoughts.
- Sign off with your full name and contact information: e-mail address, phone number, and address.
- Proofread! Don't depend only on spell-check and grammar-check (but do always use it). Ask a career counselor and friend to critique and proof, just as every professional does.

Your Cover Letter

Despite our high-tech fast-communication world, you still might actually have to write a letter to get a job. This one-page "cover" letter (written on white or ivory paper with your contact information on it) is included along with your résumé. It gives you a chance to explain why you are applying for the job, how your experience, accomplishments, and education will contribute to your suitability for the job, and why you are the best candidate. You are not writing in code, so explain your experiences.

Include a few sentences about how well you did in relevant courses that you think will help prepare you for the job. Explain your motivation for working for this employer. Be courtly, not curt. Do not be afraid of injecting enthusiasm in your letter to capture the attention of the employer. Your cover letter allows you to make meaning of your life, attract and impress the recruiter, and make your formatted résumé lively.

What to Write

Explain which job you are applying for, why you want to work for this employer, and what you can bring to them. Include technical or research skills, your ability to work, and pride in doing the work as thoroughly as possible.

In the next paragraph, explain your attached résumé. If this is your first full-time job, write that you are eager to apply your academic studies to the work world. Cite a paper or project you completed that might be of interest. If you have worked before, tell what you learned on the job in addition to your class work to show how you would be an asset to the organization. Describe how your cocurricular activities provided you with projects in which you have demonstrated initiative, teamwork, leadership, and acquired experience with technology, group dynamics, budgets, schedules, or negotiation. It you have held part- or full-time jobs, turn them into assets by explaining what you did and what you learned. This is a chance to expand the short versions of your achievements on your résumés. It is your turn to make your résumé meaningful to an employer, to stand out.

Do *not* make demands on the prospective employer. That is part of negotiation, so save it for after you've been offered the position. At the end of your letter, ask for an interview and say that you'll call to schedule one. You can write something like: "Thank you for your consideration. I'm excited about the opportunity to meet you and learn more about your needs. I will call in a few days to follow up and set a time for an interview." Make sure you do call within the week. Call every week until you get an answer. It is always up to you to make something happen.

Caution: Take your cover letter as seriously as your résumé. Have someone experienced, like your career counselor or professor, proof both your letter and résumé.

Finding a Contact

Identify the person who can hire you and write to that person. Don't settle for "To whom it may concern" or "Dear Sir or Madam." Don't place much hope in "cold letters" in response to "blind" ads in the paper. Sure, try. But it is better to go the extra mile and meet prospective employers who come to campus events and be sure to get their cards with their names, titles, and contact information. Call to check the correct spelling of your contact's name and correct title. Don't guess! No one wants to hire someone for a full-time job who is too lazy to double-check a title to get the job.

Narrow the field down to find the names of key people and organizations. How? Ask your professors and career counselor for helpful contact names. Other useful resources include alumni, professional organizations, and conferences. Begin the letter by mentioning who referred you, or say that you were impressed after hearing the speaker at a lecture or conference, or even that you heard the latest news about the organization's new plans.

You will have to write several drafts to make your letter as good as it can be. Why go to all this trouble? You have only one minute to present yourself as the kind of employee who the organization can trust with their products, patients, or clients, because that's about how long it will take the person to read your letter. You have to show instantly that you are enough like them to make them feel comfortable. If you are, it has to show on that first page, or you are out of the running. Tip: in the first draft underline the first few words of each sentence; if they all start with "I did" or "I am," then go back and vary the beginnings.

Always enclose your résumé with your cover letter—even if you already gave them one. Compare both your letter and résumé to make sure they are compatible. In your cover letter, share your excitement and enthusiasm for working with the organization. In your résumé, highlight your education, work experience, volunteering, and major projects and responsibilities. Make sure that your name and contact information—your home phone number, cell phone number, and e-mail address—are on both your cover letter and your résumé and that they are correct. Remember to follow up! Don't be passive ever again.

References and Letters of Recommendation

You will be expected to give the names of at least three references to vouch for your character, skills, and experience before getting hired. Choose people who you know best: professors in your major for whom you did great work, club sponsors or coaches, or internship or job supervisors who like you. Know that a professor will be happier to write a positive recommendation if you did well in the course and will expect you to ask for one.

List their names, titles, addresses, phone numbers, and relationship to you on one separate page, which you include at the appropriate time. Before you list their names, as a matter of common courtesy you must ask if they are willing to serve as references and will answer the interviewer's call positively. That call is likely to come just after you've had the interview and before a job offer is made.

But don't stop there; ask them to write a letter of recommendation for you, which you can also attach to your résumé and reference sheet. Hard as it is to ask at the end of a course, it is much harder a few years after graduation when the professor may have forgotten you. It always requires effort, but the benefits more than justify the time invested.

What It Takes

Ask your professors, sponsors, counselors, and/or supervisors to write a "To whom it may concern" letter, recommending you for a job. It need not be tailored to one specific interview; you can keep copies for future use as well. It is up to you to make the effort of writing a draft for them to help them to do the best job for you; it will also save them trouble and make them more willing to cooperate. In this draft, include:

- your full name, address, phone number and e-mail;
- your major, grade in their course, GPA (if it's 3.0 +) and graduation date;
- the title or summary of your paper or project, to spur their memory so they can write something meaningful about you; remember, they have hundreds of students; and
- your qualities, participation, talents, and contributions in their classes, on campus, and at work.

Remind them of your deadline and follow up to make sure they write it. Make their favor easier. Give them a large self-addressed and stamped envelope and hope that they can mail it back to you. They don't have to; they can forward their letter to your prospective employer. But if they do send you a copy of their letter, make copies! Make copies of everything and keep them safe in a plastic sheet and folder. Thank them for their efforts and report your progress back to them. You have just done the first stage of your networking process.

As you proceed in your career, always ask your current or best supervisor or client to write a recommendation letter. Begin a "recommendation" file and keep a master copy of transcripts, certificates, references, letters of recommendation, as well as any other official documents. You will be grateful for this collected information over time. I remind you again that you are likely to change careers every seven to ten years and may work in many jobs for each of them. *You* will be the *only* source of all this information. Keep it in a very safe place, or even better, in several safe places. Your college will keep only your transcript—not your cocurricular experiences, work history, or letters of recommendation. That is up to you to keep and maintain.

JOB FAIRS

College career centers conduct job fairs regularly and invite employers to come to campus to promote their companies and recruit students for full-time permanent jobs, or even internships and part-time jobs. They are free to you. Go. Go early for less competition from other students. They provide immediate or future contacts for you. Talk to the employers to find out what they do, what they are searching for, and whether there is an opportunity for you. Bring a few dozen copies of your résumés and take their vital information. Be curious, friendly, and ask questions. If you are interested, ask to schedule an interview. It all depends on you making something happen.

Look over the list of registered employers on the career center Web site or map to identify who they are and where their booths or tables are. Choose your top prospects, but also include ones that sound interesting. Walk around the fair to spot interesting booths and recruiters you might not have thought of. Talk to everyone. Introduce yourself. Say your name clearly (especially if it's unusual) and tell about your major, best subjects, interests. Practice a few opening questions: What do they do? What do they need? Are they expanding? What is it like to work there? How did you find your job? What is the next step? When can I interview for a job?

Your goal is to introduce yourself with enthusiasm—tell about your education and experience—to the organization. Demonstrate your knowledge of the organization. You might connect your major with your interests: you're a history major eager to use your research and analytic skills, or an arts major with a minor in psychology, which might tie in with the kind of focus groups the manufacturer hires.

Like real life, you get only a minute or two at a job fair to present as good an image of yourself as possible. Avoid inarticulate student-speak or slang. Minimize the use of "like" when it's meaningless. Practice sounding as if you were a broadcaster, or on a TV talk show, or a recruiter yourself.

Take the interviewer's business card if you are interested and make notes to yourself on the reverse side to keep as a memory jog. Ask the employers you are interested in what your next step should be. Give them your résumé and schedule an interview. Then, before the interview, look up the organization online so you can learn more about them.

How to Act During the Job Fair

Remember: *recruiters are there to recruit.* They want to find the best candidates to interview immediately or perhaps contact later, even weeks or months later when they will need them. They might be gathering résumés for some department that could not come to the job fair. Organizations put a great amount of effort and money into recruiting. It is usually someone's full-time job to recruit college candidates. Remember, it is business, serious business. Don't mistake it for any other kind of fair. It may be your first chance to market yourself. Learn to do it well, with a one-minute commercial designed to sell or present yourself. Practice.

Speak to the recruiter. If there's a line, wait. Don't interrupt the employer representatives or your fellow job seekers. If someone is monopolizing the employer's time, try to make eye contact with the representative to let him know that you are interested in speaking. Or move to the next exhibit and come back. Here are some tips to keep in mind:

- If you know ahead of time that one of your dream companies is a career fair participant, uncover as much information about it as you can find. A little advanced preparation goes a long way and can make you stand out among the masses of other attendees.
- If you discover a real interest in an employer, find the procedure to secure an interview. Show enthusiasm, and even ask for an interview immediately following the fair. Many recruiters plan to stay if they find potential candidates. Be one of them.
- Savvy sincerity works. Unless you're an especially skilled and tactful schmoozer, don't lay it on too thick. Don't lie.
- Eavesdrop on other conversations to learn how to improve.
- Don't just drop your résumé on an employer's display tables. Introduce yourself and make some conversation.

What to Bring to the Job Fair

Bring a folder with two dozen copies of your résumé and a pad of paper to take notes. Offer copies of your résumé to the employers you talk to and find interesting. Your conversation with them serves as your cover letter. Be sure to talk about your skills, major, best courses, and interests. Ask for their advice, experience, business cards, brochures, and a chance to interview for a job.

What to Wear to a Job Fair

By dressing more like the interviewer than like a classmate, you are giving a visual cue that you are willing to fit in. Not doing so gets more negative remarks from employers than you can ever imagine. Business casual attire is not so formal as for an interview, but casual definitely does not mean jeans and a T-shirt. Buy a business outfit like the recruiters wear. Think in terms of a medium-to-dark suit with a modest tie for males; a skirt or pantsuit with modest make-up or females. Lose the jewelry, studs, and cover up the tattoo. Look as prepared and professional as you would on your interviews.

Tip: Before the job fair, sign up for a workshop on "How to work a job fair" at your career center. You will be surprised at ways they can trigger more proactive behavior and help direct you to optimum choices.

Job Fair Follow-up

- Send a thank you note or e-mail within twenty-four hours of the meeting to say how glad you were to meet them, and include your résumé again.
- Ask for an interview or appointment to talk further.
- Call a few days after you have sent your e-mail or letter.
- Keep the appointment and arrive early.
- For the interview, dress the way managers do at their business.
- Bring extra résumés, letters of recommendation, and a page listing references (even if you already gave it all to them).

INTERVIEWING

Interview Strategies

Most college career centers offer interviewing practice. Sign up for a workshop or private session so you can learn how to present yourself well enough to land a job. Mock interviews and videotape sessions allow you to see yourself as others see you. Nothing else comes close to showing you how to improve your presentation to interviewers. It will be the fastest and most rewarding learning experience you can undertake. You must have the courage to let yourself grow.

Sign up for every employer interview for which you qualify, whether you are especially interested in the company or not. Count it as practice to understand what you and an employer want to accomplish in an interview. Their goal is not so much finding the smartest person for the job; it is finding the right person for the job. If you want the job, you will have to learn how to be that right person.

Smart and Dumb Interview Moves

15 Smart Moves

1. Look professional by dressing like your interviewers.
2. Have extra copies of your résumé without expecting anyone to have read it or to remember it.
3. Bring a complete list of references.
4. Provide letters of recommendation.
5. Bring a notebook and pen to jot down important information. Use it.
6. Be early. Learn beforehand where the interview is, where to park, and how to find the room.
7. Show enthusiasm, smile, and be positive—as if you're on a first date.
8. Speak politely to the receptionist; he or she is more knowledgeable than you might think and can tell you more about the company.
9. Bring your research on the employer and a list of questions to ask.
10. Find out whether the interviewer is from human resources or from the department in which you might be working. Vary your presentation accordingly; if the latter, show your knowledge of more specific details about the position and the company.
11. Rehearse your reasons why you should be the one they hire.
12. Volunteer relevant information about yourself without expecting the interviewer to do all the work or even to be an expert in interviewing.
13. Ask if they have any concerns about you that you can answer on the spot.

14. Ask for the next steps in the process.
15. Ask for the job.

16 Dumb Moves

1. Dress like a student.
2. Chew gum.
3. Leave your cell phone on and answer it.
4. Slump or fidget in your chair.
5. Do not look directly at your interviewer.
6. Know nothing about the company and think you can wing it.
7. Wait for a question that you really want to answer.
8. Do not explain how your courses and experience with clubs, work, and volunteering fit in with the company's needs.
9. Ask what they will do for you—money, benefits, vacation—before the job is offered to you.
10. Answer in monosyllables, say "like" many times in every sentence, and otherwise be inarticulate or slovenly in your speech.
11. Do not ask any questions about the job, responsibilities, or organization.
12. Complain about your problems or those who let you down.
13. Think that the company will definitely call you.
14. Walk out without thanking them and shaking hands.
15. Do not send a thank you note or e-mail.
16. Wait to hear from them about a job offer.

Successful Interviewing

It is the interview that opens the gate to the job. It is a human exchange between you and the employer that leads to their wanting to hire you or not. It is up to you to engender trust and describe enough about your skills and education to make the employer want you as part of the team.

Career Center On-Campus Interview Programs

Each semester, employers representing local and national organizations come to the career center to interview and recruit graduating seniors for entry-level positions. They are actively looking for candidates. Notices of these interviews are advertised, posted on the career center Web site, even e-mailed to students. Don't miss this opportunity, even if you just want information. Gaining experience in talking to recruiters will improve your skills. Your goal now? Being the one who gets the great offer.

Yes, it is more difficult for business majors, as well as engineers, scientists and artists, to interview. It is less a matter of IQ than BQ: Behavioral Quotient. For you techies, scientists and artists, all the glory lies in the work itself. It doesn't matter to you what you look like (and perhaps you don't bother much about style or grooming) or even what your social skills are. For you, life is all about ideas and making them work: that is, to *you*. However, to get a job—a good one—you have to make the shift to pitching to *them*. Presenting yourself may never have been on your top ten list before, but you must learn these skills. Your career depends on them.

In the interview, you, the applicant, must convince the interviewer that you should be hired. In the process, find out important information about the organization and the position. The interview, therefore, is a way for you and the prospective employer to see each other and exchange information in a way that can only be done in person. It's not called an "inter-view" for nothing.

The first few minutes of the interview is often the most critical. Employers are looking at and listening to you to see if you are enough like them to make them want you in their organization. That is the whole test, right there. They evaluate the degree to which you are or are not like them. Are you dressed like them? You can't wear a T-shirt and sneakers if they don't. You can't slouch or mumble if they don't. You have to demonstrate that you share interests, backgrounds, skills, and values. You have to show you will fit in if you want the job.

Your goal is to give them substantial reasons to hire you. Discuss your experience in your interview. Explain how you started, guided, expanded and achieved any of your project or assignment's goals. But you need to know what their needs and goals are to prove that you can do the job. Believe it or not, the interview is not about what they can do for you.

How do you know who they are? Do at least a half-hour of research. Go to their Web sites for cues about language styles. Observe recruiters on campus to see how they dress and talk, when they shake hands, and how formal and/or friendly they are. Try to imitate them. The interviewers will interpret this mirroring as a sign of high social skills, even if you feel awkward or fraudulent. It's just another self who can come out to present you as a viable candidate and later, on the job, as a valuable asset.

Like it or not, studies reveal that image is as important as content. Therefore, get yourself a coach to help you look and behave more professionally. Practice your opening lines with your career counselor, a club sponsor, or professor. Learn how to make an introduction: Be sure to smile, offer your hand, look the interviewer in the eye, and say, "I'm glad to meet you." Repeat his or her name, and enunciate yours clearly, especially if it is an unusual one. Everyone is nervous, but practicing helps you to deliver your answers smoothly and make contact with the recruiters. Rehearse answers to expected questions without mistaking the interview for a test. It is all about showing that you are qualified and that the employer can trust you with his or her business and customers.

℞ for Success

Interviewing is *not* a test; there is no right answer. You can't respond only in a few words. The art of successful interviewing lies in how you relate, build a bond, and establish a good fit. Employers need to know you, but they have little time. They need to determine your qualifications, leadership, initiative, motivation, goals, and personality and size you up before they move on to the next candidate. Their questions are designed to get quick snapshots of you in comparison to others. Therefore, your answers have to fulfill what they are searching for: someone they can trust with their clients and services. You have to practice presenting information about your education and personality swiftly and surely to a potential employer to demonstrate that you are the best candidate.

Ten Questions to Expect and Good Answers to Give

Q. Tell us something about yourself.

A. Beforehand, script your interest in your major, your activities, such as clubs, hobbies, and/or jobs you've held, along with experiences you have gained along the way. Think how you are different from someone who never did any of these things. Practice a two-minute review of your experience only as it relates to the organization. Tell about your experiences to prove that you are smart, creative, determined, and loyal.

Q. What are your strengths and weaknesses?

A. This is a tricky question, but it is common. To prepare, read your own résumé again; your strengths are listed right there. Learn to "brag honestly,"—that is, to be able to talk about your best characteristics, such as being highly organized, creative, supportive, tenacious, diligent, innovative, and great at making deadlines. Give one or two examples, but don't rattle on. Take your cue from your interviewer's face. On the other hand, no one expects you to tell your worst personal flaws or your inner doubts about your abilities. Instead, turn negatives into positives. Here are examples of acceptable weaknesses, which you hope the interviewer will view as strengths: fanaticism about getting details right, unwillingness to stop until the job is completed, and an eagerness to please the clients and supervisors.

Q. What do you do in your free time?

A. Your answer can't be just "hanging out." You have to show you have a life—sports, community, friends, culture, studying—and explain your roles and pleasures. Your outside life will tell interviewers that you're a confident and complete person. Remember to ask if they share these interests; this might create a bond between you.

Q. What are your short-term and long-term goals?

A. While you are not expected to have explicit job goals, you still have to answer. Have a plan rehearsed: you hope to do the job well, contribute, see where you can grow, learn, and take increasing responsibility. It is not a time to even hint at feeling clueless.

Q. Describe an experience in which you showed leadership skills.

A. Have an answer ready, selected from your campus activities, that fits. For example, describe how your teaching assistantship or your role in student boards or as an officer of an organization helped prepare you for business. Talk about your volunteer work and what you learned from helping to raise money for the walkathon. Discuss your campaign to get out the votes for a political office. In science, did you do well on a team in the lab? Did you help lead a school drama or art show? Tell about it. This is not the time for modesty.

Q. *What has your college experience been like?*

A. "Okay" may describe it, but it doesn't reveal anything about you to them. Talk about the courses in which you excelled, the areas you studied, some projects in which you were involved, and how you went about the process. Remember to ask where they went to college, what they enjoyed doing then, and whether it prepared them for their career. Try to find something that you both share—colleges, values, backgrounds, interests—so that you can build necessary social links or even begin a friendship.

Q. *Why should we hire you?*

A. Be serious. You need at least five rehearsed success stories from your classes, activities, and jobs. You have to demonstrate through examples that you are honest, responsible, loyal, trustworthy, smart, and resourceful and that you complete assignments well and on time. Describe your interest in the position and in their company, how that would make this choice fulfilling, and how you would like to contribute. Practice asking questions about them and their company so that they get a sense that you are alert and interested in their products or services and their way of doing business. They want to see that you are confident, enthusiastic, and willing to work with them.

Q. *What salary are you looking for?*

A. Don't answer this question about salary and benefits until the end of the interview, when you are more sure that you could be their choice. If it comes up too early, ask to save that discussion until later. Talking about it first is counterproductive; they do not know if you are worth much and you do not know their salary standards. All true negotiations set up the expected qualities before the costs or trade-offs. Near the end of the interview, if it is going well, the employer will ask you what you are looking for in salary. Do not give a set amount as an answer. It's better to ask for their salary range for this first job. Before the interview, check with salary guides and friends who work in the field so you will have some idea if the range is appropriate. For the most part, entry-level salaries are set, but they can be adjusted for years of experience and education. If you can meet those demands with an internship, part-time jobs, and a good GPA, you have a chance at the middle or higher end of the range. Also, ask about training and advancement.

Q. *Will you come back for a second interview?*

A. Yes. Think of yourself as passing through the screening process. Often the department conducts the first round and, if you meet their expectations, you meet with department heads, who make the hiring decision. The same interview rules apply. If you are invited back for a second interview, repeat your basic strategy, come with more in-depth examples and questions, and bring samples of your coursework or other work.

If the interviewer does not ask about the skills you have that are required for the job, what do you do? Weave them into your account, even though it might seem like you are pushing. You may have to push in order to get the job.

Ask for the next steps to their interview process. Thank them along the way. If you have been e-mailing before the interview, you can express your appreciation for their time and ask for the job by e-mail. If not, write a clear note to the main interviewer, using their correctly spelled name, title, and organization from their cards. Call back within one week to ask for follow-up information.

Ten Questions to Ask

1. What are the responsibilities of the job?
2. Can I see an organizational chart and where I would fit in?
3. Who would I report to? What is this employee like? When can we meet?
4. Is this a new position? If not, what happened to the last employee?
5. What is your organization's next focus? What new projects are starting?
6. What is your experience with the organization? What is your career like? What do you like best about your job?
7. How does the organization reward good work and advance their employees?
8. Does your company encourage further education?
9. What is the next step in this interview process?
10. Do you have any concerns about me that I can answer now?

By engaging positively in the interview, making the interviewer comfortable, answering questions, and focusing on the job possibilities, you will strengthen your chances. Remember to tell the interviewer how impressed you are with them and the company, and then ask for the job.

What Interviewers Really Want to Find Out

Employer surveys show that the following ranking of skills are most important in hiring a graduating student. Some of the answers might surprise you:

1. Your communication skills
2. Your interviewing skills
3. Your internships and work experience
4. Your GPA and academic credentials
5. The college you graduated from
6. Your personal appearance
7. Your major
8. Your work experience
9. Your computer and technical skills
10. Your experience on team projects
11. Your motivation and initiative
12. Your leadership skills
13. Your critical thinking skills

Don't come off as the obedient, passive "good student." Employers do not want students—they want enthusiastic, contributing employees who have excellent written, computer, collaborative, and oral skills. To determine how you stack up as a potential employee, they want to know whether you have had any work or leadership experience, what your studies have been like, what strengths and weaknesses you have. They want a measure of your ambition. Where do you see yourself in five years? I have even heard one interviewer ask, "If you were a leaf on a tree, where would you place yourself?" Could you answer this question without asking what the interviewer meant? His or her intention might be part of the question.

These are all strategic questions designed to get you to answer the implicit, although partly illegal, question that holds the key to what they really want to know: *Are you enough like us so we will want to make you a member of our team?* They want you to be similar to them—similar in values, intent, background, and vision. That translates to work ethic, personality, humor, and possibly even politics and religion. However, asking questions about personal issues is illegal, so you can be noncommittal if you wish. You do have to explain who you are by carefully selecting your experiences in school activities, part-time jobs, relevant interests, and internships and by showing how each project or area of involvement demonstrates your skills and accomplishments. They want to be able to trust you with their company and their clients.

Does this sound manipulative to you? If so, consider how you choose your own friends. You want them not only to like you but also to be just like you. You want friends to value, even mirror, your ideas and feelings. The more you share ideas and feelings, no matter how different you may appear on the surface, the closer you feel. There is a saying: We think smart people are those who think that we are smart. That is true. If you disagree, then think of whom you have asked for advice about which professor to study with, which courses to take, or even what movies to see. I would be willing to bet that you ask only those whose tastes and judgments turn out to be similar to yours. Why? You trust someone who validates and supports your own instincts about what to do. This is not strange behavior; it is human nature.

More About What to Say and How to Be Prepared to Participate

Before the interviews, rehearse a minute's self-presentation. Even if it feels embarrassing, ask someone to coach you; coaching will improve your delivery. You need to be able to be a walking, talking version of your résumé, (re)introducing yourself in an interesting, positive, friendly, and focused way, offering facts about yourself, what you have to offer, and how you will fit in.

In addition to demonstrating similar values, you have to continue to actively participate in the interview itself. It is not a one-way test, but a dialogue with your interviewer. You have to come prepared with questions about the company and even about the interviewers themselves. You might ask about an interviewer's experience and background, a lapel pin or corporate logo, how they celebrate success on the job, and whether the company normally promotes from within.

If you have trouble with this casual way of talking, pretend you are a newspaper reporter. Show interest by following up with questions after their statements. Ask questions such as, "How did your company grow so fast in the last year? Why did the company adopt that policy? When did you become a recruiter? Who were your mentors?" At the end of the interview, thank the interviewer.

If you want the job, ask if the company can hire you immediately. If the interviewer says the company is still in the process of considering other candidates, ask if he or she has any concerns about you so that you can explain yourself further. That way, you still have a chance to make a stronger pitch. For example, if the interviewer says that he or she would prefer someone with more experience, you can cite activities that you have participated in, offices you ran for, and projects you undertook in your classes. For example, here are some reasonable responses: "You are right. While I haven't taken any accounting courses, I did serve as class treasurer and was responsible for managing a budget of...." Or, "While I haven't worked for a computer company, I'm the unofficial techie in my group, always able to solve a difficult problem, and I typically work on the latest software. I'm certain I can perform for you."

Your enthusiastic defense of yourself will often work wonders. Remember, it's always better to present yourself assertively than to secretly hope they will discover the real, talented, wonderful you. After all, you are just beginning your career life. You can expect that you'll learn fast and grow professionally. If you feel some tension at this stage of the interview, you might ask how the interviewer got started. Who gave the interviewer his or her first break?

Take the Ball and Run

Here is an example of a dumb question and an even dumber answer that I actually overheard at a job fair:

> Job interviewer: "So, what kind of student are you?"
> Student job seeker: "Um...okay?"

The rule? No matter how poor the quality of the interviewer's question, you still have to be savvy enough to take the ball and run with it. You have to do better than a one-word answer. If you want the job, a response like "okay" is not okay. You have to continue: "I am a fine student, and I especially enjoy the research aspect. Here's how I presented my findings...," or, "I enjoy my science labs most because I am self-directed...," or "My best work comes in collaboration with others, for example." The key is to mention your best course or subject, illustrate how or why you performed well, and provide a reason or example. No matter the questions, you are the one who creates and supplies the answers. Select the traits, skills, and behaviors that show *you* off as the best candidate. You cannot count on improvisational skills when you are on the spot, unless you are an experienced actor. Rather than winging it and hoping for the best, prepare with the help of your career counselor:

- Reread your own résumé.
- Explain why and how you excelled in your best classes, papers, and projects.
- Explain the importance to you of your activities and the roles you played.
- Think of a few career choices you would like and why you expect to do well.

Learn the art of weaving examples of your experiences and skills into an interesting response. Even though it is a serious situation, smile, light up. Friendliness counts as much as neatness. No one wants to hire a grump. Be lively and interested; ask about your interviewer's experience and past. Think of an interview more as a dance than a test. If you are really interested in the job, say so. Far from sounding conceited, you will sound confident. Remember to ask when you can expect to hear from them.

Cell Phone Etiquette

1. Turn off your cell phone during interviews. Letting it ring is dumb, and answering a call would be *extremely* dumb. It is rude to even look at it. These rules, however, do not apply to the interviewer.

2. If you are waiting for a prospective employer to call you, answer your own cell phone with your full name, clearly enunciated. If you have an accent, remember to speak slowly so you'll be understood.

3. If you have a humorous, cute, or musical answering message, delete it and record a professional sounding message in its place.

Thank You Notes

Send a handwritten thank you note within twenty-four hours after the interview to everyone you met with and everyone who helped get you the interview. You can find samples in the career center. If you are extremely pressed for time or need to make an immediate connection, send an e-mail, using "Thank you" as the subject line. Even a simple note stating: "Thank you for your time. I appreciated your meeting with me and am enthusiastic about working for you." Proofread everything you write; read it out loud to make sure it sounds professional.

Your goal is to be better than average. You want to stand out from the other interviewees. Therefore, take the time to thank each person you met and mention how impressed you were with their organization. Cite something you discussed in the interview and remind them of your strengths. Highlight what you have accomplished so far and how that will translate into success in this new work environment. You can be sure that the interviewers will compare notes and letters when they meet to determine whom they will hire. It is worth all the extra work to find a great job!

NEGOTIATING

Negotiating Your First Job Offer: Do's and Don'ts

- When you get a job offer, try to get as much information as possible about what the job really entails; then, ask for a salary range. Choose high; try to get as much as you can get in salary and benefits.
- Don't take the first offer just because you are desperate or grateful. You will more than earn your salary. Try to get an appropriate salary first, even if you have to go through the tough task of negotiating for it. Make your prospective employer state the range first; don't be the first to state a number. Counter with a number 50% higher. The typical compromise is somewhere in between, so aim high.
- Know what the job is worth before the interview. Research the average salary for the job in the many resources in the career center library, such as *The Occupational Outlook Handbook*, information from online sources such as Choices or Eureka, as well as current employment salary data from the National Association of Colleges and Employers (NACE). Also, ask people already in the field.
- Postpone salary discussions until the end of the interview. If asked, say that you would like to save the discussion until the end of the interview process (if you know an offer will be made). You might say, "I am sure we can come to a fair salary agreement when the time comes. For now, I would like to tell you more about my strengths for the job."
- If the interviewer asks about benefits, ask about specific benefits. You want medical and dental insurance, a week's paid vacation, and some sick leave. You would be happy to have stock options and a flexible spending account. You would love reimbursement toward

the cost of continuing education to advance your knowledge. Even if you are tired of going to school right now, you would be foolish not to take advantage of this.

- Instead of asking for what you need, which is irrelevant to the job, ask for what you are worth based on your education, your work experience, internships, clubs, and talents.
- The truth is, however, that most people do not start out making much money. It helps to check into the average amount or to know the range; you can find such information at the career center. You will be a better negotiator if you know the going rates. Even though you would like more and need it to repay loans or to buy a new car, you are better off arguing on the merits of your degree, experience, and strengths versus what you need.
- Don't accept a low salary just to get in, hoping that once you are there, they will recognize your talents and raise your salary based on your worth. Your future salary history may depend largely on your starting salary; if you start 10% too low, you might always be 10% too low.
- Don't think you have to respond immediately to an offer. You can always say, "Let me think about it. Is this your best offer?" They may add more. Time gives you a chance to check with your counselor and friends. It does not always work, but it is worth a try.
- Make sure you have talked to the person you will work for. If there is bad chemistry, ask for another interview to get a second impression. While you do not have to love your boss, it helps if you respect him or her.
- Sometimes you will suffer from the best kind of problem: two competing offers to choose from. If one employer offers more opportunity to learn and grow but less money to start, you might risk it after checking with others who have been there before you. If an employer is in a new field or one that is very compelling to you, then take that chance. Most often, people recognize the advantages of choosing the larger, more comprehensive company with name recognition and a respected training program.
- Write a thank you note to show your appreciation, reiterate your interest in the job, and restate a few of your strongest assets that make you the best candidate.

The word "salary" comes from salt. Value yourself and be "worth your salt."

Keep a file of business leads and business cards with notes on the reverse side about the people you have met to jog your memory. This file allows you to write letters and to recognize the people with whom you are corresponding. With these contacts, you are on your way toward discovering the true heart of your work life. You may be doing the interviewing yourself soon.

If You Have a Disability

If you have a disability, the Americans with Disabilities Act (ADA) protects you. But bear in mind that not many people have experience with employees with disabilities. They might be as uncomfortable as you or more so and may not know what to say. It is always up to you to set the tone and put the interviewer at ease. You have a real chance to show your credentials and character. If you are a comedian like Kathleen Buckley, you would have them rolling in the aisles. However, if you are a serious, dedicated student looking for a great job, you have to follow all the guides for successful interviewing. In addition, you have to decide whether you want to disclose your disability if it is not evident. If you do, do not lead with it. Be enthusiastic about your coursework and activities, your dedication and creativity. Near the end, tell what special equipment you might need and how you will manage your disability on the job. If you give false answers about your health or disability, you may risk losing the job.

HOW TO FIND THE RIGHT JOB

Finding Out What You Want

Check out work environments—large corporations, small businesses, government agencies. As a rule of thumb, it is often better to start with the most prestigious organizations, which offer training, professionalism, and advancement. That, in turn, makes you more valuable when you look for your next job. Consider these things first:

- Choose your ideal location—urban, rural, or suburban.
- List three of your job skills and pick your strongest. Does it concern people, data, or things (e.g., machinery, computers)?
- Focus on what kind of reward is most important to you—money, security, creativity, or community.

Strategies for the Job Search

- *Practice job interviews. Take advantage of coaching. Be brave and smart: Ask to be videotaped while you rehearse job interviewing. Take a look at yourself, fix flaws, and retake the video to see how you improved. Learn to describe what you have learned in classes and clubs, internships and work. Tell why you would make a great employee. Don't pretend you know a lot; you are not supposed to. Ask what concerns an employer may have about you and try to alleviate those doubts. If you can't counter an employer's reservations about you, say you are willing to learn. Ask for the job.*

- *Go after jobs. Don't wait for recruiters to arrive on campus. Identify people who are written about in the newspaper or interviewed on TV. See if you can establish some link; you can even ask for a temporary job.*

- *Don't wait to be launched. Don't depend on the prestigious reputation of your college or university to catapult you into the world. The difference between students who get a great job and all those who don't is the energy and work they are willing to put into this process.*

- *Combine theory with hustle. Hustling—not the dance or any illegal occupation—is the ability to go after what you think you might want. It connects your interests and abilities to the marketplace and identifies where convergence occurs. You will learn to act for yourself, not just to fulfill assignments. It will be more fun than you think. Whether you are interested in a career in academia, science, entertainment, or sales, choosing work that you love is the best-kept secret, the juice of the real world.*

Most job growth in the United States comes from small businesses—groups with fewer than 200 employees. These small companies provide our economy with nearly two-thirds of all new jobs and revenue. Because they are constantly changing, they require more versatility. See if small business characteristics fit your needs:

- You are given more responsibility in a less restricted bureaucracy. You have to be resourceful and self-motivated when you are given more responsibility.
- You have more opportunity to share your ideas and suggestions.

- You have less job security than jobs offered by government agencies.
- Starting salaries and benefits are more variable, offering more of a risk.
- You have the opportunity to be involved in every part the creation or growth of a new company.
- You might also be eligible for stock options and profit sharing.

Researching Career Options

- Develop a list of possibilities.
- Visit your career center, interview employers who speak on campus, shadow employers in their own offices, surf the Web, and check out career books and information (i.e., *The Dictionary of Occupational Titles* and the *Occupational Outlook Handbook*).
- Identify whether your desired career requires an advanced degree.
- Find trends in the field through trade publications, news/business magazines, and papers.
- Make at least three contacts with professionals in your field through professors, friends, and family.
- Contact and meet with alumni and faculty who work or have worked in your field.

Citing Experience That Counts

- Through coursework and personal research, narrow down the career options you are considering.
- Participate in a work experience or an internship program.
- Become an active member in one or more professional associations. Find out which is best for you by asking your professors and career counselor for organizations in your field.
- Volunteer for a community or charitable organization for the type of work in your field (i.e., finance, promotion, research).

Networking—The Hidden Job Market

Most people find jobs through people rather than from ads. That means you need to know people. Who are these people for your network? They are your friends, family, professors, people you know from part-time jobs, clubs, church or temple, and even chance meetings. Your network is geometrically enlarged when these people lead you to their contacts. Whether you call it "the grapevine," "schmoozing," or "working the room," networking is simply a savvy use of our human connections. The following are some tips on networking:

1.   Ask professionals whom you meet at career events the following:

   • What do you like most and least about your work?
   • What is a typical work day like for you?
   • What are the future career opportunities in this field?
   • What advice would you give to me about trying to break into this field?
   • Whom would you recommend I speak to? Why?

2.   Ask other people whom you meet along the way the same questions, as well as the following:

   • How did you find your career?
   • How would you do it over again?
   • If you were me, what would you do?
   • Do you have any advice or leads for me?
   • Did you relocate for a great job? Would you?

3.   Tell both groups of people the following:

   • About your own talents, interests, desires
   • Some good stories about some of your classwork
   • And the kinds of projects you like to work on

Follow up with everyone, thanking them for their time and the leads, giving them some notes on your progress, and asking them other questions.

Choosing the Company

Go with the company with more opportunities. Go with the better company. Or go with your heart (or gut), even if you have to relocate at first. When you turn down offers, be polite, professional, even savvy. You may well meet these employers again and want to work for them later. Write a letter explaining that you were impressed with the company but are taking another position that seems to be a better fit for you now. Close by writing that you hope your paths cross in the future. Never burn your bridges!

Handling Rejection

No one likes to be rejected—period. However, it will happen as long as you live and as long as you take chances and ask for things. You might get four dozen "no's," but the next could be the "yes" that works. For all successful people, the odds are worth it. Besides, you can improve your chances next time by learning from the painful process of rejection. Here are some words of advice:

1. Don't take rejection personally. If too many people interview for one job, those who do not get the one job offer are not necessarily unworthy. You might call to ask what the one chosen had to offer and how you can be more competitive.
2. Apply to more than three companies. Don't "put all your eggs in one basket" and bet everything on one application.
3. Don't label yourself as a failure. Successful people think that they are learning, not failing. That attitude makes all the difference between growing and feeling diminished. It is easier to say than do, but try.
4. Don't blame the system. Complaining will only make you cynical. Learn more about the system and yourself.
5. Keep trying. Go back to the job search process and make yourself focus on new opportunities and new scripts for yourself. Many people find visualization and meditation, as well as more career coaching, helpful.

If at first you don't succeed, try, try again…each time a different way!

Chapter 9
Success Plan for Your College Years

Make the most of yourself, for that is all there is.

—Ralph Waldo Emerson

Throughout this book, I have suggested behaviors and attitudes to put into practice in both undergraduate and graduate school. I have asked people well into their careers what they would do in college if they could enter the halls of academe once more. They all agreed that they would:

- be more serious about subjects they study,
- make more friends,
- take more risks,
- find mentors,
- get more involved in college life,
- take more courses of interest,
- enjoy just being in college more,
- make better use of everything available in college to launch themselves,
- tap the full potential of the career center,
- get more involved in their major, and
- ask better questions of others and themselves.

Use the following summary as a series of checklists to motivate you to act, to spur you on when you fall into the passive-student trap, so that you can make opportunities for yourself. Benefit from the insights of past graduates, which was apparent to them only in hindsight. Remember that success starts with small steps—learning to experiment and expand. Only in this process does the essence of success—courage, care, and mission—have a chance to flourish. Happy adventures in your careering!

AS YOU ENTER: R FOR ATTITUDE

Either you can cruise through college, majoring in beer and complaining about your professors, your classes, and other students, or, you can turn your college years into the most exuberant and luckiest years of your life. It is your choice. And your choice is determined by your attitude even more than your major or your IQ. Here's how to shape your attitude:

- Expect that college will be a great experience.
- Follow your nose for interests; explore what fascinates you.
- Find professors who love what they do and learn from them.
- Join research projects to be a part of the discovery process.
- Take time to develop a skill outside of class.
- Talk to as many people as possible.
- Make friends and make time to be with them often.
- Compare with your classmates what you are reading and learning.
- Create special events, such as spending spring break with friends, celebrating after an exam, discussing science, politics, life for an evening. Invite your favorite professor to join you.

YEAR-BY-YEAR PLAN

Each year in college will present you with opportunities to shape your future. If you lay the foundation during your first year, then build on it each subsequent year, by the time you graduate, you will be prepared for a successful career and fulfilling life.

Freshman Year: Getting Oriented

- Make it a priority to succeed in your courses. Study smart; use outlines to guide you. Get to know your professors and ask how you can improve. If you are stuck, find the tutoring center on campus and ask for help.

- Form a study group with three or four other students and use the group to help you learn. Meet at least once a week. The main purpose is to help each other with course content and assignments. But, you can also buoy each other's moods; everyone feels lonely or depressed from time to time. Supportive friends mean a great deal.
- Earn and learn. Jobs can give you valuable experience, to add to your résumé, and some extra income. However, you have to weigh the value of the job—both the earning and the learning—against the time it will take away from your course work and campus activities. To find a job, apply for work-study through the financial aid office or for a part-time job through your career center. You can work during the academic year and/or over the summer. Try to find a job related to your career goals, even if not directly related to them. The more real-world experience you have, the better prepared you will be to decide whether you are cut out for a given field, and the better it will look on your résumé.
- Choose a club, sport, sorority or fraternity, and/or activity from the lists of organizations on the college's Web site, the student union, or from the campus newspaper. Become active and make friends in that club or sport, because these friends could become your primary network when you graduate.
- Volunteer activities, whether for one day or a whole semester, can be life-changing experiences in many ways. You can find them listed in the student union or in the campus newspaper. Talk to other students and find friends who share a common cause.
- Visit the career center to find out about activities geared directly to freshmen, so that you can get on track and have your questions answered. This may lead to participation in a freshman career workshop, which will help you begin your college plan.

Sophomore Year: Playing the Field

- Begin to narrow down the list of majors you are considering. Take electives that sound interesting, no matter how unrelated they may seem. Imagine getting a dream job and get involved in activities, courses, and research that will lead to that job.
- Join another club. Only spend time on these activities if they mean something to you and engage your energy. If so, increase your participation; otherwise, decrease your involvement or stop participating.

- Begin to choose topics for assigned papers from your growing list of interests.
- Talk to your professors about the courses you are taking, their field of study in general, and how you can improve or learn more. Ask for their suggestions for further study and advice about your own choices.
- Sign up for a summer internship posted on the lists at the career center.
- Begin now to investigate your chances for taking your junior year abroad, or even in another state. Find out what programs various colleges or universities offer, as well as what expenses there might be apart from the tuition. Talk to the director of the year-abroad program and ask for success stories. Ask to meet students who spent a year abroad at different locations that you might consider. For the same tuition, you can experience a place, or people, that might affect your life.

Junior Year: Getting Serious

- Take at least one internship in a field that piques your curiosity. Whether or not you get paid, test drive your career and give yourself an experience that might lead to great opportunities.
- Ask for help in linking your papers to your major interests. Ask your professors where it might be possible to have your papers published.
- Ask a professor to let you rewrite one of your papers, with his or her guidance, to learn the process of writing (even without credit). If your professor is writing a journal article or book, ask if you can help. If you get paid that's great, but even if not, you might receive credit for writing, either in the acknowledgment or with a byline, depending on the level of your contribution.
- Run for office at your club. Become involved in the state or national organization. Meet more student leaders and work on your leadership skills and professionalism.
- Attend lectures on campus for inspiration and new ideas, even in courses not in your major.
- Sign up for a class offering service learning to make what you learn in class apply directly in the field.
- Get involved in a volunteer activity that interests you.

- Visit the career center for counseling sessions, workshops, assessments, and leads for internships and jobs. Attend career events and job fairs.
- If necessary, change your major or add another one. But first, talk to both your academic advisor and career counselor. Be clear about why you want to change.
- Keep a file of information and advice you've received, as well as transcripts, activities in which you have been involved, and work history.
- Start gathering letters of recommendation from professors and club sponsors.
- Meet and speak with experts in the fields you are considering, especially if they are alumni. Ask permission to "shadow" them by spending a day watching them while they work. You might be surprised where that leads.

Senior Year: Pulling It All Together

- Use assigned papers to launch yourself into off-campus organizations that are relevant to your interests. Research what they do, perhaps in one particular area. When you have written about it, ask if you can present it to them and/or publish it in a newsletter or journal that they might recommend. During this process, observe what life is like inside to see if you want to work there some day.
- Take a résumé-writing workshop and write a sample résumé along with cover letters.
- Attend job fairs and career conferences with résumés in hand, and start collecting brochures, business cards, and most important, add people to your list of contacts.
- Take a workshop in interviewing techniques. Try being videotaped. Begin to practice the art of self-presentation.
- Get letters of recommendation now (after writing the first drafts yourself) from professors, employers, counselors, and others, while they remember you.
- Network with employers during career events, with alumni in your field, and with people whom your professors recommend. Follow up with calls to schedule appointments. Gather information about what the companies do and which ones are rated as the best places to work.

- Invite prospective employers to speak at the clubs you've joined. Interview or introduce them and take their cards. Write a thank you note and ask for more information if you are interested in their companies.
- Get an internship in the very organization where you eventually want to work; try to do your placement in what your dream job might be. It just might happen.
- Investigate graduate school. Decide to apply or not, now or later. Do not decide without talking to your professors and career counselors.
- Make time to do a real job search. Don't procrastinate then panic and settle for a job you will never like.
- Ask for interview coaching and advice in negotiating.
- Sign up for the alumni association to support your college.

GETTING THE MOST FROM YOUR COLLEGE ENVIRONMENT

In Class

Professors and Classroom Behavior: Freshmen and Sophomores

- Keep up with your assignments and studies. Avoid having to cram.
- Follow class lectures closely and ask questions in class.
- Get involved in class discussions.
- Form private study groups and meet regularly.
- Read your professors' published work.
- Find which professors are most respected, through recommendations, ratings, and books and papers they have written, and through references to their work.
- Visit professors during office hours; build relationships so you can investigate subjects that interest you and find mentors and advocates.

Professors and Classroom Behavior: Juniors and Seniors

- Find out what research or special projects are going on in your department and join in on any basis, from volunteer to paid professional.
- Ask about independent study, exchanging one class for another, increasing your load, or taking an advanced class.

Assigned Papers and Projects

- Aim to finish your assignments early, so that you can meet with your professor (or teaching assistant) for feedback on the structure and content of the work you have done. Prepare a first draft and schedule a consultation to provide you with a framework of ideas. Although this sounds impossible, you can do it. Taking these extra steps will enhance your performance in college.
- Seek out people in the field that interests you. They might be willing to act as your mentors or advisors, providing you with actual case materials from their businesses.
- Compare your papers with your classmates' work. Learn how to express ideas more cogently.
- Form a study group and learn to discuss intellectual concepts and collaborate on projects. Help each other learn about both the content and context of college and about dealing with tough relationships, both in and out of class.
- Write your papers with an extra purpose in mind. Try to publish them in a campus newspaper or magazine, or in a professional journal or a popular publication.
- Think of using your papers and assignments from various classes to explore a particular area from several different angles. Each academic assignment might then build on a concept that could be expanded into a thesis or dissertation.

Essay Tests

- Approach your professor early with questions when essay topics have been assigned. Show an outline of your answer to determine whether the substance and style are appropriate.
- Compose each answer as an entire essay with a defined beginning, middle, and end. Be sure there is a logical flow.
- Learn to think about what the facts mean instead of merely reciting them by rote. Discover what recognized theorists believe and form your own opinion, whether you agree or disagree.
- Discuss your exams afterward with your professors to find out how you can improve your answering style or where you went wrong or misunderstood. The point is not to change your grade, but to learn to think more clearly.
- Take notes during or immediately after these sessions; it is easy to forget what is said, especially if criticism is involved.

Standardized Tests

- Find as much as you can about the test in advance. Learn about the format of the questions and what content will be covered.
- If you intend to apply for graduate or professional school, investigate which admission tests are necessary, when and where you can take the tests, and when the test scores are due to the admissions office along with your application. Get samples of the tests. Start studying well in advance of the test, whether you are studying on your own or taking test preparation courses, which often are available on your own campus.

Outside of Class

Professional Relationships

- Get to know your advisors and staff to find out information about special programs, financial aid, grants, internships, and work-study opportunities. Introduce yourself. Ask questions. Read bulletin boards. Participate in events. It is why you are investing precious time and money to be in college.
- Make it a point to meet the dean of your school formally by attending open meetings and lectures, as well as informally by stopping by during office hours. Familiarize yourself with the administrative structure of the college.

Clubs and Activities

- Discover the array of available activities—debate, orchestra, literary journal—from the student organization office, other students, and professors. Visit the first meeting of several clubs to see which are most interesting to you. Then join.
- Find ways to become active. Volunteer for a committee.
- Build an area of expertise within a club, and commit yourself to deliver what you have promised. You might sample several clubs or specialize in one club or activity and take it to the limit.
- Experiment with different aspects and roles such as supporter, leader, director.
- Develop strong relationships with the sponsor, faculty, and staff responsible for that activity.

- Find business, arts, and service contacts outside the campus, all of whom might be interested in your club's activity.
- Make friends with classmates older and younger than you. Ask the older ones for advice about classes and careers. Advise the younger ones in return.

Work

- Find a job that interests you, hopefully one that relates to your major. Start with excellent performance even in the most menial tasks. Once you prove your loyalty and competence, you might be able to advance. Do not be shy about using connections and asking about opportunities and for help when you need it.
- Think of a job as a social experience and take time to meet employees and clients.
- Treat each job as if it were your own business. Think of how you would run it in terms of product quality, management, employee motivation, customer relations, and profit making.
- Find existing internships or create your own, on or off campus. Find out what other students have done and learn from their experiences.
- Find opportunities to meet local business or professional people; talk about your experiences and ask about theirs.
- Work as a teaching assistant to gain experience in speaking and lecturing.
- Work as a research assistant in a laboratory, or on a project, if you are interested in developing ideas, working with a team, or are considering graduate school.
- Work on campus and learn how a college works. Find mentors among administrators, who know the system and will share that knowledge with you.
- Pay as much attention to the way you work with people as you do to completing the task itself.

Career Counseling Services

- Go to your career center early and often to discover what it offers.
- Establish a friendly relationship with career counselors. When they have helped you, let them know it. Suggest other means of assistance, and volunteer to make arrangements if necessary.
- Find out what interests you; then explore the field with ideas from your career counselor.

- If you do not know what you want to do, ask for help. Investigate several different fields to see which beckons to you. Try to find a related internship.
- Take workshops and seminars to learn what professionals do as well as to discover or confirm your interests.
- Start your own placement file with letters of recommendation from professors whose courses you have recently taken and excelled in. It may help if you draft a letter for them, although this might be difficult for you to do at first. Ask a career counselor to show you some sample letters of recommendation. Make copies, but keep the originals in a safe place along with diplomas, transcripts, birth certificate, licenses, and your social security card.
- Sign up for interviewing sessions. Have your session videotaped. Ask for coaching to improve your presentation.
- Use every opportunity to interview with recruiters, even if you are not totally committed to their company or field.
- Contact alumni in your field of interest for informational interviews, advice, and job leads.

Strategies for Getting Recruiters to Offer You the Job

- Show up on time; you do not get a second chance.
- Dress for the interview as if you had the job. Look like them.
- Think through answers beforehand to such questions as:
    1. Why do you want this job? Do your talents and interests fit your major?
    2. What skills do you have? Technical, leadership, teamwork?
    3. What experience do you have in activities? Responsibility for funds raised, sorting out conflicts, initiating projects?
    4. What did you learn from your courses? Critical thinking, rewriting reports, working on a deadline, learning new and complex theories?
    5. What are your biggest successes in college?
- Talk through answers, giving some examples from your experience with professors, sponsors, coaches, and bosses in class projects, extracurricular activities, sports, and clubs. They want to know that you are responsive, educated, and enthusiastic.
- There are no "right" answers in an interview. It's not that kind of test, but you do have to show that you can be an asset. What counts? Telling what you did, how you did it, and what you learned

in your time in college, during summer or winter breaks, on your part-time job, in your clubs and activities, on your own. Accomplishments to list are, for example:

1. Organizing a Habitat for Humanity weekend
2. Volunteering on a college recruiting panel for high school students
3. Running a campaign to elect a candidate for student government
4. Serving on the debate team
5. Taking a semester' study in another country
6. Writing a sports column for the campus paper
7. Learning to sign for the deaf
8. Serving on a research team for your professor

- Ask about what they are looking for and whether they have any concerns about you. Answer immediately. But if you cannot alleviate those concerns now, you can send your responses along with your thank you letter.
- Combine hustle with theory. Success calls for active skills in networking and connecting so that your interests, abilities, and job requirements converge.
- Learn how to develop ways to act for your own well-being, not simply to fulfill assignments like a robot.

Chapter 10
Making the Transition

Whatever you can do, or dream you can, begin it. Boldness has genius, power, and magic. Begin it now.

—Johann Goethe

CAREER TRENDS

Where the Job Market Is Headed

Your major may not lead directly to a career.

It may surprise you to know that most graduates are not working in fields directly related to their majors. Do not worry. They did not choose wrong majors at all. What they studied in school is just not focused on a career. Often your major does not end up defining the course your life takes, and when that happens, you must determine what will. The answer lies partly within you and partly in finding satisfying opportunities. It now becomes your task to learn how to match your own evolving skills and interests to opportunities; and those discoveries can become your internal passport to exciting new worlds—of work, that is. Formulating your career compass is not so easy to do now, let alone in the unforeseen future. But, if you are willing to do the hard work, it will pay off in so many different ways, from finding what makes you happy to securing a job that can support your lifestyle.

Expect to return to school more than once.

If you are like the vast majority of professionals, you will no doubt join the throngs of people, at every stage of their careers, going back to college or graduate school for new degrees, licenses, and certificates, as well as for new or advanced professional training. As information and the world of work evolve, and as you change and grow, you will need and aspire to more training to stay current, credible, and curious. If you employ the lessons of this book and take charge of your education while in college, then the transition to the work world will not be so drastic. Because, from graduation on, you are solely responsible for managing your career—what you need to know, how to educate yourself, how to harness your ambition and desire so that you can continually update your skills to meet the demands of the workplace.

Expect to change jobs and even careers many times.

More than ever before, people change jobs and careers. Some change jobs from necessity because their old jobs evaporated, were incorporated into other jobs, or their workload increased unbearably. Other people are motivated less by status or money but more by a search for greater meaning in their lives. For example, some people who want to abandon the fast track to lead simpler and/or more family-oriented lives are willing to move to smaller towns to start over, or they find fulfillment by building meaningful relationships in their neighborhood in the city. As others on the career track rethink what fulfillment means, they begin gathering like-minded people together in support groups.

Why? Such revolutionary change has been going on since the 1970s. A person's work life used to be fixed, secure, and predictable. Most people in your parents' and grandparents' generations knew what to do, what was expected, and how to advance and succeed. But, over the past three decades, four radical changes profoundly reshaped the employment landscape, breaking down monolithic structures and blurring what people took for granted:

- Corporations have been merging and reorganizing at an unprecedented pace. One-half of all corporations listed in the 1970 Fortune 500 list have vanished. Many of those that survived have modified themselves beyond recognition. From the mid- to late-1990s, to the time that followed the burst of the economic bubble in 2000, the labor market resembled a rollercoaster. The marketplace revived and exploded into new services, new products,

and new ways of doing business. More small enterprises were created than ever before, many founded and operated by women, as
well as men, experimenting with employee leadership and ownership. In today's work world, employees of small businesses now
outnumber the employees of all the Fortune 500 companies.

Many larger organizations started challenging their own
meaning and methods. Mission statements were conceived and
formulated by employees. Businesses and people used to know
exactly what they were going after: immediate profits and maxi-
mizing efficiency through standard operations were the key factors. Now such organizations are more customized. Businesses
and people are now suddenly open to experimenting, open to
looking around to see what might be a good fit. Those answers
often mean going global and forming alliances with former
competitors.

Entire industries are morphing and collapsing old boundaries. For example, the entertainment industry, which used to be
separated into distinct areas based on format, such as television,
film, radio, and music, is now almost without boundaries. It now
comprises markets such as video games, computer graphics, mer-
chandise, real estate, theme parks, and banking. Artificial divisions are giving way to more organic forms and alliances—locally,
nationally, and globally. One multinational company owns
Disney Concert Hall in Los Angeles, Disney movies, Disney
World in Florida, and Disneyland amusement parks in California,
Europe, and now in China. That kind of diversity under one corporate umbrella did not exist forty years ago.

- Computers revolutionized information access by 1990. This revolution shows no sign of slowing, thus forcing out old systems
and the people who managed them and bringing in new systems
at a rate of change measured in months.

- Globalization and internationalization are proceeding faster
than ever. These movements are typified by people moving
around the world and becoming familiar w   countries and cultures, transforming them into world citizens. b t the cost is high.
As organizations change to meet new and evolving markets with
more demanding stockholders, they are focused even more on
profits. To do more with less, they outsource work and hire more
temporary, contractual, and part-time workers, often without
paying benefits. Workers or employees, on the other hand, have

to keep growing and learning—to depend on their networks to find jobs, and to manage their own careers and their money. Even though these new skills have not yet been taught in college, those migrating into the workforce must learn how to take care of themselves.

- Organizational structure has become much more fluid and less rigid. The old pyramid structure, borrowed from World War II's military model, was a fixed hierarchy in which the few at the top created plans that were implemented obediently by the employees waiting for their orders. In exchange for your loyalty, top-down companies offered life-long job security, no matter how much you did or did not enjoy the work. That type of organization has given way to a new model, which is more organic, more like a spider web, more flexible, yet more chancy. While in this new type of work world, you have no promise of employment, neither are you stuck in a job that does not fulfill you. The concept of work becoming your personal fulfillment is a radically new idea.

Millions of mystified and angry workers have been displaced just when they thought they knew their jobs and their places. Even middle managers and clerical staff have been suddenly scrambling for the unemployment lines, reading classified ads in newspapers, journals, and online job listings. You might have lived through this yourself; maybe this was a factor motivating you to return to college. Or perhaps you witnessed your parents or an older sibling caught up in the angst of losing a job and not being able to replace it.

Hardly anyone has been spared in this new, aggressive environment. Whole departments and divisions can be fired, downsized, or, euphemistically rightsized. The disorder spreads like a virus. In nearly every industry, most people have to work for new bosses, sometimes every 3 or 4 months. That means that many have no chance of retiring naturally after a long term of service, but are abruptly fired. Companies sometimes outsource jobs to other countries to achieve lower labor costs and then hire employees back as temporary workers without benefits.

Change is powerful. We have not escaped it, not at work, and not at home. "No-fault divorce" occurs every day in business. Those who lose their jobs, much like those who lose their spouses, lose their very identities and must search for more than just work; they are looking for themselves. Many learn the cost of depending on an outside system, whether the split is from a corporation or a marriage. Then they learn the twin skills of self-reliance and team collaboration, and they learn them the hard way.

I have witnessed people changing entire careers, not just jobs, as often as each decade. Change means constant modification, even reinvention. The old adage, "Do well in your job and the company will take care of you," simply no longer applies. You have not only to do well, but also to manage your own career. You must prepare yourself to learn and thrive. You are off to a fine start by deciding to go to college as a preparation for—and an important part of—life. Start developing your skills for success in college.

Don't be too afraid that the first job won't last. Many jobs will have a short tenure, which means that people will continue to move in and out of the company. Moving or switching jobs no longer carries the old stigma of "job-hopper." Everything changes, including jobs. The marketplace will. Best of all, you will. You are starting the first part of your first career. There is no set map to find your way to the next part. Thankfully, you do not have to settle for less than you had hoped for, either in opportunity or rewards. Wherever you start, it is up to you to pursue a fulfilling career. Advancement or change can come through following a hunch or from a great project, or by following a great boss who is promoted and takes you along. Or you may find a position that is newly created. Or you may decide to go to graduate school and follow a different track. Or you may discover a new aspect of a project, another project, or a whole new area that absorbs you totally.

Technology has drastically changed the place where many people do their work. Some people telecommute, working from home for their companies, and connecting through e-mail and the telephone. While some virtual workers admit to missing the comments of friendly coworkers, others welcome the lack of interruptions. Record numbers of people are starting their own home businesses or consulting services.

Top 10 Skills Employers Want

No matter who the employers are, they all agree on which qualities are important in their employees. They all want to hire people who possess the following ten critical skills, no matter if you ask recruiters or the National Association of Colleges and Employers:

1. Communication skills
2. Work experience
3. Motivation and initiative
4. Teamwork skills
5. Leadership abilities
6. GPA/academic credentials
7. Technical skills
8. Interpersonal skills
9. Analytical skills
10. Ethical behavior

How can students develop these skills? It is no mystery. To cultivate these desired traits requires you to give up playing the passive role of obedient student. It requires you to become more actively courageous—to search out the endless opportunities that lie within the academic curricula. In turn, you will also learn skills for success in the real world.

More specifically, employers are looking for personal traits, such as:

1. Can you think creatively and critically?
2. Can you work collaboratively and cooperatively?
3. Can you speak and write clearly?
4. Do you have the flexibility to manage diversity in the workforce and with clients here and globally?
5. Do you have a good general education, as well as good computer skills?
6. Do you show a strong work ethic?

Launch Your Own Career

Where you go to college may not matter as much as you may think it does. Successful people in many different fields have told me that it matters less where you go to college than the amount of positive energy you put into what you do while in college. Sure, going to Harvard or Stanford might help you get a better first job. And, yes, having a Wharton MBA or a Yale law degree or a Ph.D. from UCLA gives you an advantage for getting your first job with the most prestigious corporations or agencies.

Even if your school's reputation and connections get you in the door, there is no guarantee that the degree will keep you there. Prestigious labels by themselves will not make you who you want to be or take you where you may want to go. Studies reveal that only half of college graduates believe that they are using their full occupational potential. A college degree, in itself, does not launch your career, even though it may be a great predictor of your field of professional work. You have to launch your own career. No matter where you have matriculated, small college or large university, private or public, single gender or mixed, you can discover yourself and your talents and turn them into a series of opportunities that will start you on your future success. You can make your dreams come true.

HOW TO MAKE A SUCCESSFUL TRANSITION

The transition from college to the work world is one of the most dramatic changes you will ever make. Entering the "real world" with your first job, you may experience confusion and anxiety. You may not get an orientation program. Here are some prescriptions to help you transition successfully from school into your career—no matter what organization hires you.

Rx 1: Change Your Attitude

As a student, your responsibility is to respond to exactly what your professors ask of you, and you are graded immediately. Rarely are you asked to rewrite a paper or retake a test to improve. You never have to persuade your professors to advance you to the next stage; if you do what is expected, you are automatically promoted. But the work world is different. On the job, you will be working for supervisors and coworkers who expect you to perform at a level of high competence. You will be promoted only when you exceed expectations, and sometimes not even then. Therefore, you have to shift your attitude from expecting to be advanced routinely up the career ladder to recognizing that you must be willing to learn as much as you can in each position you hold and promote your own advancement.

Rx 2: Change Your Behavior

In college you probably have been able to cut class at times, sliding in late, or arranging a class schedule to fit your social and sleep habits. But now showing up on time every day is definitely a minimum expectation; you do not receive extra credit for punctuality. And while you may have kept to yourself in a class or lab, now you have to modify that loner behavior. Even if you are not a natural extrovert, you will have to make the effort to fit in at your new place of employment. Being new is never easy, but it is important that you take the initiative with your coworkers. Begin by introducing yourself to everyone. Greet people, shake hands, tell them where you are from, and ask them about themselves—who they are, what they do, how long they've been with the organization. After the conversation, jot down the their names and what you learned about them. This will help you learn who everyone is and acclimate to your new environment. Do not enter into any cliques; get to know as many people as possible. Since it is too early in the game for you to understand the workplace politics, it is better to be open to everyone.

Rx3: Change Your Talk

At your new organization you may be working with people close to your own age, but you will also be working with people your parents' age or older. They will, no doubt, come from different backgrounds, follow different religions, and enjoy various types of entertainment and food. These differences are what make human interaction so interesting. Be open to learning about your coworkers. It is, however, important to keep in mind that in the workplace successful employees adopt a "language" that helps unite them with their coworkers and maintains professionalism. This language includes a more formal manner of speaking than you may be used to. Learn their language. Notice how your coworkers and boss talk to each other. Use their professional communication as a guide for how you should speak with your colleagues, administrators, bosses, and clients. Also, don't complain, don't backstab, and be as professional as possible.

Rx4: Change Your Learning Habits

Learning opportunities were abundant and clearly defined when you were in college. Professors gave you textbooks, curriculum overviews, learning guides and outlines, labs, discussions groups, and projects. Now that you are working for a living, you will learn in different ways. As you start your new position, you may be overloaded with learning tasks. But once you establish your daily duties, the responsibility of continuing your education will be up to you. Ask coworkers and supervisors for feedback on your performance. Hone your skills and broaden your knowledge by taking continuing education classes, joining professional associations, and reading recently released journals and books related to your field. You will have to think ahead to know what you will need to learn and who can be powerful mentors in this process.

Rx5: Change Your Interaction

You will probably become frustrated with parts of your new job. That is normal. Everyone does. How you handle that frustration, however, is what really matters. You will need to solve tough dilemmas, deal with difficult people, and act ethically, all while keeping your cool. You can always ask for advice or help. Your coworkers and supervisors know more about the job than you do, so don't be afraid to learn from them. And if you mess up on the job—which is also going to happen at some point—be mature enough to take ownership and apologize, rather than being defensive. Make up for it, if possible. Don't forget to learn from the mistake so that you can do better next time. Start complimenting great work and behavior; you will learn more yourself and make friends too.

Rx6: Change Your Focus

Keep in mind that your written job description, if there is one, is only the bare minimum of the actual job requirement. Pleasing your boss, making him or her look good, now becomes a top priority. During your first few days and weeks on the job, be observant—find what your boss really wants from you and figure out ways that you can deliver. Instead of waiting for assignments, stay a step ahead by finding ways to contribute without always being told what to do. For example, if you have some spare time at work, forget about making a personal call or paging through a magazine; make yourself useful. Learn about your company—its history, services, products, and clients. Think about how you can contribute to its success and to yours. Make yourself visible on the job. Build relationships not only with your peers, but also with your bosses. Write memos to demonstrate your knowledge and highlight your work. Volunteer for task forces or special committees. Speak up at meetings in a positive way.

Start small. Initiate informal conversation with your boss, or even your boss's boss, whom you might meet casually in the elevator or parking lot. Ask a question and/or make a comment, but do not complain or backstab. Attempt to get to know the people in your company through their interests and talents. Do the best you can and ask for help when you need it.

R_x7: Questions to Keep Asking Yourself

- What part of this work is interesting to me?
- How can I better use my strengths?
- What stops me from learning more or relating better?
- How can I advance or start again?

> We know what we are, not what we may become.
> —Shakespeare

THE NEW MEANING OF SUCCESS

You Must Change

College commencement is literally our moving on—to the world of work, to a full-time career. *Career* is a more accurate word than *work*. *Career* implies something more significant than simply performing one task for pay, just so we can live. For most of us, our work is a large part of our identity. We experience life through our own framework, and the work we select guides how we think, what we learn, who we know. Members of each profession, for instance, scientists, view the world differently from the way artists or corporate managers do. What we do becomes who we are in such a profound sense that we feel that we have found our *calling*. Our work, then, becomes our gift, one that we feel intensely alive in, one that we pursue for our lifetime.

These past few years you have been living and thinking of yourself as a student, and maybe unconsciously you view yourself as not quite fully adult, responsible, or self-sufficient. The time has come to make an enormous leap toward a new identity.

Many of us resist change, because adapting to a new, unknown set of circumstances is uncomfortable and often produces anxiety. New situations can be difficult to live through. Prepared as you may be, you can't direct or stop your emotions. Everyone who changes goes through a psychological shift. The discomfort of transitioning from college can be made easier if you can develop the skills you'll need beyond college while you're still in school. The more you experience and risk, the more open you are to life, the greater your likelihood of finding what you are searching for.

New college graduates yearn for security and order and are seeking companies and professions that just might provide stability. A response of caution is understandable.

You will likely define success on your own terms, perhaps beyond money or status. You want to be able to match your work to your interior yearnings. Don't deny those yearnings. Of all your accomplishments identify which ones give you a sense of pride. Fusing your passions with what you do best and what you most want to do in college will help you translate that passion into a professional career. Maintain close relationships with your family and friends, find mentors, and create community activities that connect and nourish you. If you are intent on living to the fullest, take time to explore what it means to be true to yourself. After all, you will be changing and growing as long as you live. Take time to begin your career in college and prepare for your first job. Build your activities, courses, and internships into a résumé for success.

Psychological and emotional values are now part of the work equation. We have discovered that we have the power to change direction to reframe what we call work. More and more, we have been giving up our dependency on organizations. Even when stressed or anxious, many have been starting over as free agents—consultants, solo owners, or entrepreneurs, either by themselves or as members of small consortia. We yearn to find meaning in our lives, finding our calling in our work, so that our work activities are congruent with our truest missions.

The Parable of the Talents

Consider this version of the biblical Parable of the Talents. A master called his three servants before him and gave them "talents"—the old word for currency or coins. Then he went on a journey and left them with their talents. The first servant gambled his and lost them all. The second servant, afraid to risk his, buried them. The third servant invested his talents and multiplied his share. After a long time the master returned and asked his servants what they had done with their talents. When he heard from the two first men, he was displeased with them for wasting or hiding their talents. He rewarded the third servant, who invested his talents wisely.

But exactly how do we develop our own talents and invest them wisely? Successful people serve as fine models; their lives show how to answer this question. They have enhanced their careers by developing both technical talent *and* nontechnical skills. And in enhancing their initial talent, they have contributed to their professions. These are skills that you can learn and practice now.

The Learn–Do–Teach Cycle of Careering

This cycle, if followed through with a spirit of commitment, results in the most successful careering. We proceed through three stages in our lives: to learn new ideas and skills, to practice and master them, and then to teach them to others. Moving through the complete process gives us perspective and understanding, as well as a system for involvement in our work and in our own lives. Without this kind of growth, we stay stuck, perhaps as perpetual students or dissatisfied workers. Avoid living "stuck," like a broken record, by moving through stages of careering to replenishing ourselves. We must frequently reconsider what we have learned in order to go forward in our present endeavor, or to begin a new one. Then we need to practice whatever it is that we have set out to learn until we have mastered it. At that point we can pass our experience on to others. The penalty for not moving is that we hinder our potential and limit our ability to change or adapt to a new situation.

> *Most people have work that is too small for their spirits.*
> — *Studs Terkel*

FINAL NOTE: THE NEXT MYSTERY IN YOUR LIFE IS HOW TO BE FULFILLED IN YOUR WORK

Life is at its best if you are doing what you love, what you think you are born to do. If you can identify what that is, you can make an intelligent move in that organization, no matter how menial the first job is. If you have no idea what turns you on, get a job in the best company you can, and learn from it. For you are at the beginning of a life search: Begin an exploration of what goes on in every department and see what attracts you.

In the twenty-first century, most adults will hold multiple jobs in their lifetime. Very likely, no job will last forever. Your first job may be simply a lead to another one. Unlike college with its linear prerequisites, working is far more of a dynamic multidirectional adventure. Embrace it.

Work is quite different from what you might expect. It is more than the sum of its parts, beyond just doing your assigned job. It is about risk, loss, gain, politics, negotiations, rewards, occasionally even betrayal, and finding and fueling your ambition. You will learn what interests you, who inspires you, and how best to cope with disasters and enter the phase that follows them. Your learning curve is about to rise.

If earning a diploma cannot guarantee a certain kind of life, with a whole lot of school, work, and family in the middle, then what purpose does college serve? It is to learn how to think, how to extend your mind, how to get involved and research information. It is a time to learn to develop social skills, and also a great time for experimentation. The point is that we change all the time, as the world changes. College is a beginning point, and the very meaning of graduation is commencement!

Make learning a personal and lifelong activity; make it your motto. If you are alive, you are never finished learning. Ask your professors for advice. Send for graduate school catalogs. Apply to a variety of programs. Ask about fellowships, grants, and specialized programs. Consider night or weekend programs for pursuing your graduate studies. Don't allow yourself to stop. The sky is the limit!

My life's work has been devoted to helping people find their callings, pursue their passions, and make their lives rewarding. I have found that each of us is inspired, nourished, encouraged, and confirmed by loving support from others. We are, in addition, emboldened and transformed through our will to try, to take a chance. Everything is open to you—if you are willing to go for it. To begin, just begin. For if not now, when will you?

Recommended Reading

Astin, Alexander. *What Matters in College: 4 Critical Years Revisited.* San Francisco: Jossey-Bass, 1997.

Astin, Helen S., and Carole Leland. *Women of Influence.* San Francisco: Jossey-Bass, 1999.

Bateson, Mary Catherine. *Composing a Life.* New York: Grove Press, 2001.

Bolles, Richard N., and Mark Emery Bolles. *Job Hunting on the Internet.* 2ⁿᵈ ed. Berkeley: Ten Speed Press, 2005.

Bolles, Richard N., and Mark Emery Bolles. *What Color is Your Parachute? 2005: A Practical Manual for Job-Hunters and Career Changers.* Berkeley: Ten Speed Press, 2005.

Figlar, Howard. *The Complete Job Search Handbook: Third Edition: Everything You Need to Know to Get the Job You Really Want.* New York: Henry Holt, 1999.

Gibran, Khalil. *The Prophet.* New York: Knopf, 1923.

Keirsey, David, and Marilyn Bates. *Please Understand Me: Character and Personality Types.* 5ᵗʰ ed. Del Mar, CA: Prometheus Nemesis Book Co., 1984.

Phillips, Jan. *God at Eye Level: Photography as a Healing Art.* Wheaton, IL: Quest, 2000.

Scheele, Adele M. *Career Strategies: A Guide for the Working Woman.* New York: Simon & Schuster Fireside, 1994.

Scheele, Adele M. *Skills for Success: A Guide to the Top for Men and Women.* New York: Ballantine, 1996.

Seligman, Martin. *Learned Optimism: How to Change Your Mind and Your Life.* New York: Free Press, 1998.

U.S. Department of Labor. *Occupational Outlook Handbook, 2004-2005.* Indianapolis: JIST Works, 2004.

Index

Note: Page numbers followed by sb indicate text found in sidebars.